CONTEMPORARY COMPOSERS
EDITED BY SCOTT GODDARD

ILDEBRANDO PIZZETTI

Other titles in the series

MAURICE RAVEL by Roland-Manuel

BOHUSLAV MARTINU by Milos Safranek

SERGEI RACHMANINOV by John Culshaw

ERIK SATIE by Rollo H. Myers

In preparation

VAUGHAN WILLIAMS by Percy M. Young

ALBAN BERG by Willi Reich

JOHN IRELAND by Philip Radcliffe

WILLIAM WALTON by Nigel Townsend

CONTEMPORARY COMPOSERS

*

GUIDO M. GATTI

Ildebrando Pizzetti

London

DENNIS DOBSON LIMITED

FIRST PUBLISHED IN GREAT BRITAIN IN 1951 BY
DENNIS DOBSON LIMITED
12 PARK PLACE ST JAMES'S SWI

Translated from the Italian by
David Moore

PRINTED IN GREAT BRITAIN
RICHMOND HILL PRINTING WORKS
BOURNEMOUTH
138/R

Contents

I   The Life   9

II   The Stage Works   15

III   The Choral Music   62

IV   The Songs   76

V   The Chamber Music   83

VI   The Orchestral Works   92

VII   Critical Writings   103

VIII   Conclusion   108

Appendix (a) A List of Pizzetti's Works   116

(b) Bibliography   120

List of Illustrations

Ildebrando Pizzetti, 1949   *frontispiece*

Pizzetti as a student at Parma, 1898   *facing page* 16

Pizzetti at the time of 'Fedra', 1911   32

A page from the autograph of Symphony in A   48

Stage design for Act III 'Fra Gherardo', La Scala, Milan, 1928   64

Pizzetti at Locarno with Riccardo Bachelli (left) author of Il Mulino del Pol and Guido M. Gatti   80

Stage design for Act III 'Orseolo', Florence, 1935   96

Pizzetti at work at his piano   112

Introduction

THE NAME OF Ildebrando Pizzetti has long been known not alone in his own country but abroad, and his work held in honour. Whenever one hears something new of his, and for us foreigners his works are so rarely given that there is continually something 'new' to hear, one has the experience of listening to an individual, a live mind, a real personality. We would willingly hear more; but the trickle from Italy remains sparse. His larger works we only know by report. This is especially the case with his operas.

The condition of opera in England today is one of enthusiasm often misdirected, of hope perpetually frustrated by lack of means both artistic and financial. It is therefore not surprising that Pizzetti's *Fedra*, *Dèbora e Jaéle*, *Fra Gherardo* and *L'oro* have not yet appeared in London. Economic storms do not induce an atmosphere favourable to the production of contemporary operas; in so wild a climate only favourites deeply rooted in tradition can hold firm, and so survive. And since under a puritanical system of travel restrictions few can get to Italy, or having got there can afford a ticket for an opera performance, the likelihood of hearing a work by an important contemporary such as Pizzetti recedes into a distance peopled by millionaires and diplomats.

Yet we in this confined island can at least receive from abroad news of what we are constrained to forego at home. And having had our appetites sharpened by these reports of unheard operatic delicacies can find, perhaps, sufficient strength to hold on until the night when an opera by Pizzetti is produced at Covent Garden or Sadler's Wells.

Such news of later works than the operas by Donizetti and Verdi recently produced in London by the Teatro alla Scala is to be found in this volume.

The author brings to his task of elucidation and comment the two valuable attributes of enthusiasm for Pizzetti's music and thorough knowledge of it. It need hardly be said that the two often exist apart. But only when they combine, as they do in this instance, does that peculiarly hazardous act of describing music by means of words provide the reader with what he wants, a technician's expert guidance enlivened by the communication of an individual enjoyment. To these qualities the author adds personal knowledge of the composer. Thus admiration of the music and the man go together.

The larger part of the analysis in this book is taken up with opera; inevitably so since Pizzetti is an Italian and therefore, one may say, an operatic composer by right of birth. But the reader who turns to those chapters that deal with the chamber works, the songs and the choral works will discover that Pizzetti's mind, naturally stimulated though it is by the stage, is also deeply moved to expression in other styles of composition.

Signor Gatti has no difficulty in bringing Verdi's name into the discussion of Pizzetti's musical ancestry. 'To Pizzetti,' he writes, 'the maestro of Busseto is the prototype of the artist-man...' He assures us that Pizzetti has 'felt that Verdi's imagination was fed by sentiments that are deeply rooted in the human spirit—simple, primitive sentiments, which can be understood by all, of whatever country or period'. Speaking of Verdi's *Messa di Requiem*, evidently with reference to Pizzetti's work of the same name, Signor Gatti remarks that Pizzetti 'is a more cultivated, more thoughtful artist [than Verdi] who has lived in an age more given to reasoning, and as a result his vision is broader'. By which the author means, I take it, that as a man Pizzetti is of a more complex fibre than Verdi; which may well be true. In the end musicians are judged by their work and the time is not yet to compare the work of Pizzetti, a living composer, with that of one whose work is ended. The value of the author's comparison of these two mentalities is that it brings Pizzetti into direct line of descent from Verdi and shows that he does in fact belong to that great tradition.

SCOTT GODDARD.

CHAPTER I

The Life

THE LIFE OF Ildebrando Pizzetti has not been markedly adventurous. Indeed, it has been singularly lacking in external events. The most important dates are those of the *premières* of his works, which constitute the climax of the long and wholly internal labour of creation. The characteristics of the artist are repeated in the man, who is loth to talk about himself, and does not like to advertise—even by unobtrusive and subtle propaganda—or to allow others to advertise his work, still less the facts of his ordinary existence—ordinary, that is, in its outward manifestations. In his personal life too it is impossible to detect changes of direction or tendency during the course of the years. I at any rate cannot point to any, though I have known him, roughly speaking, for upwards of thirty years.

Pizzetti was born in Borgo Strinato, Parma, on September 20th, 1880. His father Odoardo was a teacher of the pianoforte, and when the little Brando was two years old he moved with his small family to Reggio Emilia, where he had obtained a post as a teacher of solfeggio in the Scuola Comunale di Musica. At Reggio the boy went through his elementary schooling and lived in a musical environment, but his first love was the theatre; his earliest ambition was to become not a great composer but a famous dramatist. Music *per se* was something to which he would turn his attention later, if at all. For the present he thought of it, or so he felt, in terms of the theatre. He wrote several plays, or rough drafts of plays, two of which he saw performed in 1894 by a group of actors whom he had himself gathered together, choosing them from among his schoolmates. One of these plays was entitled *Odio e Amore* and was taken from a French novel. The other, which was actually inspired by Silvio Pellico's *Le Mie Prigioni*, was called *La morte di un prigioniero nella Rocca dello Spielberg*. This theatrical work did not, however, prevent Pizzetti from being a diligent scholar—one who profited from the study of the classics, as his subsequent work clearly reveals. (Actually he was twice punished while he was at the Gymnasium, the first time because he was found copying out a part from one of his plays during a lesson, the second for refusing to attend classes in gymnastics—'two punishments', he himself remarks, 'which, alas, did not cure me of either failing'.)

At the age of fifteen he entered the Parma Musical Academy, but since his family was still at Reggio Emilia he spent several years going to and fro from one town to the other. Later on he lived at Parma with his grandfather Innocenzo, who took a delight in hearing him play works by Rossini and Bellini, Donizetti and Verdi, and fortified himself with a sublime patience and resignation when he practised works by Wagner or classical or modern pieces. The years 1895 to 1901 were years of study and research, of discovery and disappointment; but all the time Pizzetti revealed a determination to rise from the slough of mediocrity and to be worthy of those artists—many of them from his own city—whom he admired and loved. He studied instrumental and choral works, in particular some of those which Italians have forgotten, at the Academy, which from the end of 1897 onwards was directed by Giovanni Tebaldini, a man of taste and culture as well as courage. He listened to theatre music in the Teatro Regio; the gallery in which he used to sit was often transformed into a battlefield, for it attracted a multitudinous audience of impressionable and excitable working-men, quick to give their support but ruthless towards the artist who failed in his duty, even for a single instant.

In his book on Pizzetti, Tebaldini dwells at some length on his pupil's activities. They were by no means insignificant, as we may appreciate if we merely think of the number of compositions which Pizzetti submitted for the annual proficiency-tests. The final test in the academic year 1897–8 included a performance of his 'symphonic paraphrase' of Victor Hugo's poem *Extase* (actually the title and the idea of using the poem as a motif were suggested by the master, for they had not even occurred to his pupil at the time when he composed the piece at Coviolo in the spring of the previous year). The reporter of the *Gazzetta di Parma* discovered in the composition 'conspicuous and important qualities which now lead us to predict for Pizzetti—if he continues to apply himself steadfastly and assiduously to his studies —a very brilliant future.' In the following year he submitted two pieces for the test—*Il sonno di Giulietta*, a symphonic interlude (after Shakespeare), and a *Canto di Guerra* for chorus and orchestra (based on the fourth canto of *Fingal*). Already there is a suggestion of the theatre, for the two compositions are fragments of operas which Pizzetti may have completed, drafted or merely envisaged. (This was the period of his collaboration with Annibale Beggi—a period which he has so vividly recalled in the oft-quoted preface to his *Intermezzi critici*.) The year 1900 witnessed the completion of a *Sinfonia campestre*, of which only two movements were performed at the Academy—the adagio and the scherzo, entitled respectively *A sera nei campi* and *Mattino d'aprile*; a Sonata in C minor for violin and pianoforte; and a few pieces of sacred music. However, late in October of the same year Pizzetti, together with the rest of the students from the Academy, went to Busseto for a concert arranged by Tebaldini on the occasion of the eighty-seventh anniversary of the birth of Verdi; and at Sant'Agata he saw the maestro. This is one of the events which have made the deepest impression on the artist's mind, one that he still remembers as vividly as if it had occurred yesterday. A group of young students entered the grounds of the villa and waited. After a little while the glass door opened and in company with his guests, towering above them all, there appeared Giuseppe Verdi. 'I had the impression', Pizzetti was to write thirteen years later, 'that a complete silence had suddenly descended on the scene. Very rarely, either before or since, have I had such an impression of universal religious awe.'

During the academic year 1900–1, his last at the Academy, Pizzetti was put in charge of the quartet class. For the proficiency test he submitted a Trio in G minor for pianoforte, violin and violoncello; the *Ouverture per l'Edipo a Colono*, which, though its style is somewhat reminiscent of Beethoven, must, in virtue of its precise melodic design and its atmosphere of gentleness and warmth, be regarded as the first typically 'Pizzettian' composition; and a *Canzone a maggio* (after Politian) for solo voice, chorus and orchestra. In July 1901, he obtained his diploma in composition with the traditional pieces—a motet for five voices (*'Pater si non potest hic calix transire'*), the first movement of a sonata for violin and pianoforte, and a lyrical scene (after R. Salustri's *Ruine di Braunia*) in which he employed a form of recitative written in a seventeenth-century style which was destined never to recur in his work.

Having left the Academy he was unfortunately obliged to think of the realities of life, the problem of which was by no means easy of solution. Owing to the death of Professor Crotti the post of librarian and professor of the history of music in the Academy had fallen vacant. Wishing to compete for it, Pizzetti set about writing an exhaustive historical and critical work on the musical tendencies of the time. He also contemplated an essay on Schumann, studied the music of Bellini and, in an effort to discover the right road, sought to make himself conversant with artistic questions of every kind. Meanwhile he devoted himself to private teaching, turned his thoughts to the theatre and, so as to be in closer touch with it, agreed to act as assistant to Cleofonte Campanini, conductor at the Teatro Regio. In addition to the *Tre Preludi per l'Edipo Re*, the Quartet in A for strings and the songs, to which further reference will be made, he composed a Trio for oboe, horn and pianoforte, a Mass for four voices, strings and organ and the symphonic poem *Canente* (after Ovid), none of which has been published.

One day in 1905 he read in the review *La Lettura* a fragment of the prologue of *La Nave*, which d'Annunzio was then writing. Finding that the verses seemed very suitable for modal treatment, he set them. This music he sent to the poet, who replied to his third letter by offering him his congratulations and commissioning him to write all the other music necessary for the work's performance. Ildebrando da Parma, as d'Annunzio, *more solito*, renamed his young collaborator, finished the work in the summer of 1907, but the first performance of the poem did not take place until March 1908.[1] This was the composer's 'official' baptism.

[1] At the Teatro Argentina, Rome. The conductor was Vittorio Gui.

He remained at Parma for a few months longer—he had meanwhile been engaged since 1907 as a teacher of composition at the Academy, where he had also held for some time the chair of musical history—but having been selected for the post of teacher of harmony and counterpoint at the Instituto Musicale, Florence, in the autumn of 1908 he moved to that city, where he remained for almost sixteen years, as a teacher until 1917 and then as Director of the Instituto. These were the busiest and most brilliant years of his life. At Florence or, during the summer, in the heart of the surrounding countryside, he wrote the whole of his first three operas, the two sonatas, the songs, *La Pisanella*, the choral works and the *Messa di Requiem*, as well as planning some of his later works. Dividing his time between home and the Instituto, his family, his pupils and a small but trusty circle of friends, he passed his days in an atmosphere of profound tranquillity. He lived for a short time in Via Spontini, then in a street behind the church of the Madonna della Tosse which was known at the time as Via Pancani. Later he had a house in Via dei Serragli. The largest of its many rooms overlooked a garden and was his studio. Maria Teresa and Bruno, his children, had plenty of space in which to play, and Bruno, if I am not mistaken, even had his own little room where he kept the puppet-theatre of which he was so proud. (And there was also Signora Maria, kindly, smiling, solicitous, who was destined to die there almost without warning in November 1920.) Pizzetti played an active part in the musical life of the city, founding in collaboration with Ernesto Consolo that 'Society of Music-lovers' which was to be the breeding-ground of a series of larger enterprises. He used often to take part in learned and fruitful discussions with the members of the *Voce* clique and with Papini, Bastianelli and especially, De Robertis. In association with Bastianelli he undertook the publication of an anthology of modern music, *Dissonanza*. Only three parts appeared, but they included some excellent pieces by composers who, in those days, did not easily find publishers and backers.

In 1924, having been appointed director of the Milan Conservatorio, he regretfully left Florence, remaining in Milan until 1936. In that year he was summoned to fill the chair of advanced composition at the Accademia di Santa Cecilia in

Rome, where he is living still. Here too he divides his time between the school, his home—where his life is enriched by the companionship and love of Signora Riri and his affection for his youngest son Ippolito—and the Accademia Nazionale di Santa Cecilia, over whose destinies he presides.

CHAPTER II

The Stage Works

THE PERSONALITY OF Ildebrando Pizzetti as an artist is intimately bound up with the problem of musical drama. This is the fundamental problem arising out of his poetic doctrine; it enables us to solve the equation of his work and to discover the secret of his creative genius. Theory and practice are interwoven and merge into one. If we were to consider Pizzetti's work in its separate manifestations and its development we should at once perceive—even if its creator did not himself tell us so—that its essential nucleus is to be found in the body of his dramatic compositions. But we must be clear from the start as to what we mean by the terms 'dramatic' and 'theatrical' in order to avoid ambiguity. When I use the words 'drama' and 'dramatic'—and they will often recur in the pages of this book—I do not mean to refer merely to the works that Pizzetti has written for the theatre. What I have in mind, on the contrary, is a particular conception of the work of art that is peculiar to him, a style which he has made his own and which is more or less apparent in each of his works and, I would say, in every action and at every moment of his life in so far as the latter finds its complete expression in art. Could any art be more intensely and profoundly human than the dramatic art? 'Not merely lyric writing, *i.e.* something which springs from those momentary and transient feelings of exaltation which nevertheless have their *raison d'être* and are themselves expressions of a life that is at bottom unconscious, nor even merely epic composition, signifying the objective representation of visible reality, but drama, *i.e.* life in movement, action.'[2]

[2] I. Pizzetti, *La musica nella vita italiana contemporanea*, in *Atti dell'Accademia del R. Istituto Musicale 'Luigi Cherubini' di Firenze*, Anno LIII, 1917.

Thus the problem of musical drama, which, from the time of the Camerata Fiorentina to the present day, has been raised in every form and solved in every way and, what is more important, has been at the root of so many outstanding works of art, tends to become indistinguishable from the general æsthetic problem— that of the ceaseless and imperious moral demands of the artist, which are exalted and likewise satisfied.

An invaluable source of information on the development of the notion of drama in Pizzetti's mind is provided by the 'dramatic autobiography' which he wrote by way of a preface to the collection of essays entitled *Intermezzi critici*. In this work he relates how, almost from childhood, he delighted in opera, which he idealized and loved in one work after another by the most famous lyric dramatists of his day until he had a clear, and in his eyes unexceptionable, vision of his own. Pizzetti tells us that this vision was the outcome not only of critical reasoning but of many and varied creative experiences which he turned to good account. 'When we come to consider æsthetic problems we cannot, I think, discover and benefit by the truths which lie behind them merely by critical understanding and the use of reason. Experiment is essential; and if we take the wrong road the consequences of our error will lead us to seek the right one again and again until we have found it.'[3]

At the age of seventeen, that is in 1897, he collaborated with the poet Annibale Beggi, his bosom friend, in writing the opera *Sabina*, based on an Alsatian legend. This work 'conformed in structure to the conventional notion of an opera. It was full of echoes of all the musical compositions that I had studied and was extremely unsophisticated, with much incoherence of form, grandiloquent language and ostentatious emphasis.' After making an attempt, which was at once abandoned, to write an opera based on Murger's *Bureurs d'eau*, he produced in 1899 a *Giulietta e Romeo* in which there was already something which *Sabina* lacked—'a certain consistency of treatment and method, in other words of æsthetic purpose'. But above all the young composer's first encounter with the lofty dramatic poetry of Shakespeare had served to create in his mind an ever more beauteous vision of 'that problem of drama whose solution or

[3] *Intermezzi critici*, p. 11.

16

Pizzetti as a student at Parma, 1898

elucidation he now regarded as the supreme goal of his artistic activity'. In 1902 he went in for the second Sonzogno Competition for a one-act opera, contributing *Il Cid*, based on Corneille and Guilhen de Castro. This opera, which was disqualified from the contest because it lacked a final scene, was indisputably modelled on an up-to-date conception of the great melodramatic works of the nineteenth century—'the drama being composed from beginning to end of melodic flourishes, the scenic opera being concentrated in a series of lyrical effusions in the style of Rossini, Bellini or Verdi... but [the whole] enriched by a new and more varied vocal and instrumental technique... a versification no longer so regular and straightforward as theirs, but bolder and more varied... a new song-formula equal to theirs in power, movement and beauty, but freer in rhythm and metre'.[4]

At this point the composer's vague and contradictory attempts and experiments came to an end, and he embarked on the road which henceforth he was never to leave. *Il Cid* 'was the experience one needed in order to demonstrate in the best possible way that lyric and dramatic writing are two different things (although the latter includes the former), and that if one so much as ventures into the maelstrom of lyric utterance one is carried so far from the path of drama as to be in danger of never finding it again'. Naturally it is not asserted that, once the composer had established his basic principles and concentrated his researches in a single direction, his immediate essays completely fulfilled his aspirations, for as he gained in experience so he became a more and more severe judge of his own work. The years from 1903 to 1907 saw him conceive and reject the idea of a *Sardanapalo* (from Byron) and a *Mazeppa* (from Pushkin). In addition he attempted an *Aeneas* (from Ovid) and a *Lena*, but abandoned them both, the first because the subject was lacking in humanity, the second, which had a contemporary setting, for almost opposite reasons, namely because it depicted 'a situation so obviously real, so recognizable and identifiable as such, that the author would have been denied all scope for the use of his imagination, while in the mind of the spectator any expressive power that the music contained would have been reduced and perhaps destroyed'.

[4] *Op. cit., passim.*

But the plot of *Lena*, which was wholly invented by the composer and his friend Beggi (who combines with him to form a single identity), decisively reveals to us his moral predilections. He sketches here the first lines of that human 'character' which subsequently he will strive to probe ever more deeply and to represent in fuller detail. Already his choice of subjects had given some indication of his preferences. The period with which we are concerned embraces the last years of the nineteenth and the beginning of the twentieth century. Naturalism was at its zenith. The *bourgeois* drama was predominant in the theatre, and the realist opera was the beacon on which young writers almost without exception had fixed their eyes. Italy was still resounding with the success of Mascagni's *Cavalleria Rusticana* and Leoncavallo's *Pagliacci*—a success that was not so much unusual as unique. Puccini's *La Bohème* was first produced in 1896 and *Tosca* in 1900. In France the sympathies of Massenet's admirers were divided between *La Navarraise* and *Sapho*; Alfred Bruneau was preparing to introduce into the lyric theatre the characters of Zola's novels, while Charpentier was dreaming of the society opera and championing the cause of all the Mimi Pinsons of suburbia. From this point Ildebrando Pizzetti personifies the reaction against this *embourgeoisement* of stage types. We have seen that he borrowed his characters from Shakespeare, Byron and Corneille, and as soon as he had chosen them and gathered them about him he exalted them to the level of his ideal, selecting 'episodes that were almost commonplace, but capable of assuming a lofty and universal significance'. In *Lena* the essential characteristics are clearly defined: 'Two central figures—on the one hand a man in revolt against the laws and customs of contemporary civilization in the name of new ethical principles, which he senses instinctively rather than comprehends through the power of thought, and on the other a woman, Lena, who, defying the laws of her fathers and rising above the new social principles of her lover, affirms and demonstrates the pre-eminence of a single divine law—the law of love.' We already have here the dramatic knot which will unite Deborah and Jael, Gherardo and Mariola, the Stranger and Maria—though the implication and intention will be totally different. Is this an affirmation of religious faith—religious not because it is mystical or somehow transcendent, but because it signifies the acceptance of life in purity of heart, with its evils to which one has to oppose, so far as one can, a resolution born of love? It is that same anguish which will cause Jaéle's voice to tremble as she faces Dèbora: 'And you, you who feel no compassion/for the woe of mankind,/are you quite certain that you understand clearly/the will of God?' It is the anguished doubt which in Maria (*Lo Straniero*) will become certainty: 'I feel that your God,/that God Whom you seek and will find, is great/ and just and holy, more so than your evil gods,/and even more so than my father's.' For this faith she dies in joyfulness of heart, and with her the Stranger dies as well, 'that he may teach men to love'. Service and love—the truth which inspires Fra Gherardo before he ascends the funeral-pyre (and in each case it has required a woman, a humble creature of pure sensibility, to reveal it to disillusioned eyes): 'Give without asking/and love, love, love!'

In these circumstances it was natural that the composer should focus his attention on Greek tragedy, which he had already considered and analysed from the dramatic and musical point of view. Being an ardent admirer of Gregorian plainsong, which he had traced back to its sources, he had studied with great devotion and insight the music of the Greeks (later he was to treat of it in a historical and critical synthesis which is still one of the pithiest and most vivid pieces of writing that any artist has produced on the subject), and its richness and variety of mode had furnished him with many suggestions. But more than the comprehensive range of Greek tragedy, which he deemed to be essentially an epic and lyrical form of expression, and hence far removed from his dramatic ideal, what had struck him was the stature of its heroes, who were an expression of the loftiest universal human values, and the original collaboration of the chorus, a complex and variable character, whose sensibility and re-activeness were in aggregate equal, if not superior, to those of all the other personages. The seed fell on favourable and well-prepared ground (many writers, including Pizzetti himself, have referred to the influence exerted by popular songs of the Emilian plain on his early development) and was soon to yield fruit of the most delectable kind in the music for Gabriele d'Annunzio's *La*

Nave. With one exception these pieces were choral and, apart from the *Inno a Diona*, religious, or rather liturgical, in inspiration, being written in the modes of Greco-Latin music.

Among the Greek tragedians he concentrated on Euripides, from whose works he chose *Hippolytus*. He wrote part of the libretto and read a few pages to d'Annunzio. The latter, who was then writing his *Fedra*, advised him to wait until his own tragedy was complete. When Pizzetti had become acquainted with it he felt it to be so 'in keeping with his intuitive conception of the human and divine being' that he abandoned his script in favour of that which the poet, 'in a brotherly and generous spirit', offered him. In this way *Fedra* came into being. Composed between 1909 and 1912, it was performed at the Scala, Milan, on March 20th, 1915, Gino Marinuzzi conducting and the chief parts being interpreted by Salomea Krucenisky, Fanny Anitua and Edoardo di Giovanni.[5]

In Euripides the figure of Phaedra does not emerge into the full glare of the limelight, since she is an intermediary rather than a protagonist in the conflict between the two adversaries, Venus and Hippolytus. We do not know the tenor of the libretto which Pizzetti had derived from the Greek tragedy, and hence we do not know whether he had built the plot around the enigmatic figure of the daughter of Pasiphaë or whether he had instead preserved the relative positions of Euripides' characters. But the important thing now is to note how d'Annunzio's tragedy, apart from those features which do not altogether conform to Pizzetti's notion of the drama (as we shall shortly see), and despite certain situations which have led some to regard the work as immoral, anti-Christian and calculated to arouse unhealthy passions, corresponds in its inmost meaning to Pizzetti's ethos as revealed especially in the final scenes. Above all, it is as far removed in spirit from Euripides' tragedy (and even from those of Seneca and Racine) as was Pizzetti's conception. In Euripides, Phaedra is represented to us as a victim of fate, of an occult power that is superior to the human will, a power that she cannot even fully comprehend. In d'Annunzio, not only is the heroine aware of the drama in which she is involved—indeed, she is merciless in her

---

[5] Edoardo di Giovanni was none other than Edward Johnson, later manager of the Metropolitan Opera House, New York.

20

analysis of her every gesture—but she succeeds in triumphing over it, certain of her immortality and conscious that she will achieve victory through death. The victor in d'Annunzio's tragedy is not fate but the human creature. It seems to Phaedra that her misfortune is the expression of another reality which altogether passes human understanding and that her guilt is measured by a law which summons that reality into the field of man's experience: 'My name is ineffable—like the name of him who overthrows ancient laws that he may establish a mysterious law of his own.'

We have reason to believe that these were the traits in d'Annunzio's heroine which struck the composer and made a lasting impression on his sensibility. Those who have marvelled at the way in which Pizzetti passed from the Greek world to that of the Bible, transferring his affections from Phaedra to Jael, have not sufficiently pondered the fact that in d'Annunzio's tragedy, and still more in Pizzetti's opera, the character of Phaedra contains elements of Christianity in the broadest sense of the term. If Aethra and Deborah belong to a world still governed by Fate and Law, and submit voluntarily, even with a passionate conviction that they are in the right, to a power stronger than, as well as extraneous and almost hostile to, the human will, Phaedra and Jael, in proclaiming aloud their victory—in the former's case over the divinities Venus and Artemis, in the latter's over the stern dictates of the Mosaic Tables and of the official priests—become the champions of a conception of the world that is altogether different, being closer to ours and in any case the only one offering possibilities of dramatic development. It is easy to see that Pizzetti is at such pains to stress these traits in the protagonist's character that in the event his interpretation has become as unlike d'Annunzio's as it is possible to imagine, even if the poet did accord it the sanction of his complete approval.

In practice, the collaboration between poet and composer was cordial but difficult. Pizzetti, who was young and unknown, had some scruples about suggesting to d'Annunzio cuts and modifications in the text. But although the number of lines had been reduced by about half the libretto of *Fedra* was still very different from what the composer desired, as is evident if we consider the following passage, which contains in a nutshell his dramatic credo:

21

By the term 'musical drama' I mean—and I am profoundly convinced that in saying this I am proclaiming an incontrovertible æsthetic truth—not merely a drama in which every episode, every detail of the action, every gesture and every word uttered by the characters may find in the music the expression that is necessary before they can be fully understood by the spectator, but also one in which the music is rendered capable of revealing continuously the mysterious inner working of the human soul in a measure that is, and always will be, beyond the scope of words. The function of poetry in musical drama should be to bring about this revelation, or better still this translation of feelings into the language of music. In conclusion, the musical potential of a drama is identical with its capacity for being so translated. Now the poet can realize this ideal musical drama only if he makes it consist, so far as the action is concerned, solely of the episodes necessary for its development, in other words by stripping it of any episode in which music cannot play any other part than that of an adjunct, accompaniment or commentary, and if he reduces the verbal self-expression of the characters to the words that are necessary for the intelligible manifestation of their hidden feelings, that is to say by eliminating from their conversation every element of psychological self-analysis. Music that is an adjunct or simply an accompaniment to a drama only has the effect of needlessly protracting its development and of rendering it less intelligible; and a superfluity of words in the expression of feelings has no other effect than to hamper the free development of the music and to minimize its efficacy. There is no æsthetic reason, no law of contrast or anything else that can justify the presence in a musical drama of an episode that is not so important as to be necessary. And there is no lyrical consideration that can justify the verbosity of a character who expresses his or her feelings by a subtle and exhaustive process of analysis... [6]

But if in *Fedra*, considered in its entirety, we do not yet discern the typical Pizzettian musical drama, conceived and expressed as a single entity and corresponding in its every aspect to the ideal to which the composer aspired, the opera nevertheless embodies for the first time his characteristic and personal modes of expression and that vocal and instrumental language of which he was to make a close study and which, though he raised it to an ever higher pitch of fluency and responsiveness, he never ceased to employ. It is obvious that in *Fedra* the composer does not yet enjoy to the full that freedom of movement which he will be able to achieve only when poetry and music come into being within him simultaneously, as in *Dèbora e Jaéle* and subsequent operas.

[6] In an essay on P. Dukas's *Ariane et Barbebleue*, in *Rivista Musicale Italiana*, XV (1908), pp. 87-8.

Generally speaking, words are still an encumbrance both in themselves and by virtue of the fact that they are constantly expanded into lyrical images. In such cases Pizzetti's musical interpretation of words is perfect, but it cannot be said that the general arrangement, structure and dramatic rhythm are not at times adversely affected. D'Annunzio, who was endowed with a prodigious verbal sensibility, saw this clearly when he declared that in the entire score of *Fedra* 'not a single note is at variance with the spontaneous rhythm that graces every line. Indeed, each note makes the rhythmic group of words with which it is associated more expressive without dislocating or distorting it'. But in this scrupulous fidelity to the text lay the very danger which the composer succeeded in avoiding at moments of maximum dramatic intensity or, as in the finale, of complete lyrical catharsis.

As to the orchestration of *Fedra*, it furnishes us with a happy example of rich and lively symphonic composition which succeeds in creating a background but does not seek to engage the listener's whole attention by assuming the leading part in the drama, as happens in Wagner. Let me not be misunderstood if I speak of orchestral atmosphere. The orchestration is never static or colouristic, it does not create moments of spell-binding suspense, save at the end of the drama, as is just. Its elements are derived from the drama, but the latter does not unfold within it and through it. What I mean is that the thematic instrumental components never become actors in the drama, and their evolution, intrusion and completion only serve to fill out the words when these are no longer adequate and require to be translated into the language of music. If, therefore, *Fedra* contains themes, or fragments of themes, which appear with a certain frequency, they by no means have the function, either rational or literary, of Wagnerian *Leitmotive*. As an example, the tortuous theme of Phaedra's passion [see p. 24], which occurs in the first bars of the opera and intrudes itself at intervals throughout the first act, will never reappear as the dominant theme even though that passion actually reaches its highest pitch in Act II. It is a theme that came into being as an expression of a phase in the drama, and Pizzetti feels that its renewal at any time after that emotional phase has been superseded would be dictated not by any fundamental necessity but by a conceptual logic which to

him is anathema. (The same may be said of the successive appearances of single motifs, which are never developed or modified harmonically in the ingenious manner of Wagner.) The orchestra does not present itself in the form of a close tissue of themes. On the contrary, it is a coherent organism, with an independent existence alert and sensitive to every nuance of the drama, and without pauses and irrelevant symphonic interludes. It does not include fragments of rhetoric capable of standing by themselves, such as we find in d'Annunzio's poem. For it is impossible to regard as such either those passages whose character was frankly episodic even in the poem, nor indeed those others which by virtue of their actual position—at the beginning or the end of an act—could easily be detached from the remainder. The composer was fully conscious of the poem's organic life, and disregarded emotional incidents that stand on their own 'like loose pearls'. When *Fedra* first appeared its language was described as 'musical prose'[7] because of the absence of strophe and rhyme. Indeed, if we consider it from the purely technical aspect, we can speak of it as prose—beautiful prose, measured and resounding. But seldom was prose more sublime, more vibrant and more richly leavened with poetry. As has already been said, the composer let slip no opportunity of raising the tone of the narrative, which in some passages of the poem becomes merely illustrative or stagnantly descriptive. But he certainly has not substituted musical rhetoric, which however is so much simpler and more dangerous, for the rhetoric of the poetry, as other 'intoners' of d'Annunzio's poems have done. I would say rather that the more the text tends to lapse into the rhetorical and the

[7] G. Bastianelli, *La crisi musicale europea*, p. 184 and *passim*.

emphatic, the more careful the composer has been not to indulge in a spate of 'uncreative' sound. An adequate example of the first case is provided by the scene in which the Suppliant Women appear; this is the first scene of the drama and from the musical point of view one of the most emotional. In the vestibule of the palace of Troezen, facing Aethra, mother of Theseus, are the Mothers of the Seven Heroes, 'Suppliants with ribboned tresses and dark robes, 'twixt light and shadow'. Each of them, and all in unison, lament and bewail the deaths of their sons, employing phrases which in the poem have a cold, literary sound. Pizzetti has instantly entered into the spirit of the drama and expressed the grief of these mothers in accents that are profoundly human. We hear no distraught cries, no wailing; instead we are aware of an inward perturbation, a weeping of the heart, a tragic lament which affects us more than any grandiose 'gesture'. So restrained and appropriate is the attitude of these mothers that they seem as though they had been taken from a classical frieze, but the words that they utter have acquired a warmth which makes us share their suffering and experience their drama. Running through the entire scene is a smooth, continuous motif that is

developed, as it were, against the background of one of those rhythmical pedals, with reiterated notes, which composers often employ as though to express the beating of the heart in moments of emotional crisis. [See example p. 25.]

As to the second case, consider again the swift and violent episode—but here too it is a restrained violence, the essence of which is its depth—of Phaedra's appeal to Venus (Act I). Here it would have been so easy to become rhetorical—if we look closely we see that we are concerned with a most dramatic confession and a consummate act of self-revelation on the part of the heroine, and with a most merciless analysis of her incestuous delirium. It would have been so easy to lapse into the emotional and the melodramatic. Here too Pizzetti has not allowed himself to be diverted from his vision of the drama as a united whole, and the episode has not assumed undue proportions. The exposition becomes more emphatic, and the attitude of the protagonist throws light on her character; but there is no consequent slowing down of the insistent rhythm of the action. There are other instances of self-revelation on the part of Phaedra, and all unite to create a character that finds its full meaning in the final scene. We see clearly, I repeat, that the Phaedra whom from the first Pizzetti saw and loved is the Phaedra of the last scene, a Phaedra who has been transfigured by death and who smiles upon the stars 'at the onset of the Night', a Phaedra who is adumbrated more than once in the score even before the third act is reached— for example, in the apostrophe to the mother of Hippomedon, which throbs with a secret nostalgia inspired by feelings of maternal tenderness, a nostalgia so typically Pizzettian because of the relationship between voice and orchestra; or in certain inflexions, containing elements both of chastity and of sensuality, but of a sensuality that is almost free from the taint of sin, during Hippolytus' delirious sleep (Act II). I hesitate to cite further passages from the opera, for it would be hard to pick out another that is more unified and self-contained; but I cannot refrain from mentioning the heightened sensuality of the scene in which the Theban slave-girl is stabbed by Phaedra with a hair-pin, the account of Hippolytus' struggle with the horse Arion, the rude excitement of the last scene of Act II, when Phaedra, crazed and hate-maddened by the repulse she has met with, denounces her

step-son, the inexpressible emotion of the funeral elegy for the dead Hippolytus, which is a paragon of modern Italian choral work, and the whole of the last scene from the point at which the drama, together with all the characters, inanimate objects, actions and words, is transfigured and seems to be exalted to a different plane. Phaedra has just spoken words of reproof to Procles and has enjoined him to remove the two spears from the side of the lifeless son of Theseus; and we hear in the orchestra the soft, unearthly quavering of an E flat and, simultaneously, the theme of Phaedra's death, which sounds, however, so sweet and slow and serene that no death could seem less painful and more like a new dawn. [See p. 27.]

Pizzetti did not wait for the first performance of *Fedra* before turning his hand to a new theatrical work. In 1914 he chose as the poem for his new opera another tragedy by d'Annunzio, *La fiaccola sotto il moggio*, but after a year he interrupted the work of composition, which was already far advanced. Thereafter *La fiaccola sotto il moggio* and poems by d'Annunzio or others were ruled out. The scenes which he had written of *Gigliola* (this is the title that was to have been given to the opera, from the name of the virginal heroine, the one flower in the midst of a welter of corruption and decay—fresh evidence of the artist's ethos, which was by this time an essential part of his vision) were condemned and destroyed without hesitation or regret immediately Pizzetti realized that if he followed the path indicated by d'Annunzio's æsthetic he would never succeed in translating his own dramatic theory into reality. And since he saw no other poet or hack-librettist who was capable of collaborating with him in a spirit of brotherhood—perhaps only Beggi could have given him what he wanted—he found himself faced with the unmistakable necessity of writing dramatic poetry for his own music, in other words of creating his drama in its entirety. At first he set about this task with some reluctance and with justifiable trepidation, but gradually he came to regard it as more and more worthy, alluring and unavoidable, like that of composing the music—among other reasons because the latter came to life in his mind simultaneously with the words, and the characters in a drama appeared before his mind all at once, complete with their musical attributes, so that the rhythm of syllables and notes was one and the same thing. The libretto of *Dèbora e Jaéle* was written in 1915-16, and the score was completed on June 12th, 1921.

If the reader considers the sources—which I have indicated —of the young Pizzetti's operas or of his essays in that field he will not be surprised at the subject chosen for the new poem. Pizzetti had been acquainted with the Bible for many years, and he delighted to contemplate its heroes, with their 'superhuman humanity'. When I questioned him about the origin of the opera he wrote:

The origin of *Dèbora*? First, the need and the desire to create characters that I could 'love', characters that would be noble, pure, inspired by worthy sentiments and passions, and then the long-cherished desire, which subsequently became a firm resolve, to express in my own words that wonderful Biblical world in which, I feel, all of us, all over the world, can find our prototypes, with our passions, our aspirations, our vices and sins and faults, and our sadness, our wretchedness and our hope.

It is clear from this that the libretto of *Dèbora e Jaéle* was inspired not merely by one or another precise page or passage in the Bible but by the Bible *as a whole*. For the characters that are entirely invented by the dramatist are no less authentic, in a spiritual sense, than the rest. Through the study of texts and commentaries, of historians of the Jewish people and Jewish thought, but above all by means of his infallible poetic intuition, Pizzetti has conjured up the Biblical world with an intensity and clarity of outline which even scholars have esteemed highly. The raw materials and historical subject-matter of the dramatic poem are, to be sure, contained in Chapters 4 and 5 of the Book of Judges, where there is an account of one of the numerous episodes in the war between Israelites and Canaanites, which had persisted for several generations—to be precise, throughout the so-called era of the Judges. But what a transformation this material has undergone! An episode which in the Bible was a combination of the epic and the lyrical has become essentially dramatic, and under the influence of their passions the characters have acquired a human and therefore dramatic coherency which they certainly did not have before. In the Old Testament Deborah and Jael are spiritually identified with each other. Deborah is she who commands in the name of the Lord and Jael is one of the instruments of the divine will (although it is not made very clear in the Scriptures why the Kenite's wife suddenly slays the fugitive king after receiving him hospitably in her tent). There Deborah and Sisera stand face to face. The struggle is a struggle for power; hence it is expressed above all in external events. This is the spirit of the Biblical story. The Lord hastens to the aid of His people, despite the fact that they have broken their Covenant, when He sees clear signs of remorse and penitence. Whoever has trusted in God will triumph, and the man of Belial, the idolater, will be utterly destroyed.

In Pizzetti's poem, on the other hand, if Deborah and the Israelites generally still conform to the Biblical pattern, Sisera and Jael diverge from it to a pronounced extent, the more so as at one stroke they are raised to the dignity of protagonists, whereas in the Bible—and this is especially true of Jael—they merely serve to reflect the character of Deborah. In Sisera and Jael Pizzetti has created powerful, vital dramatic personages; he has pictured the spiritual crisis with which they were confronted, and the rift which opened up in the soul of each between passion and duty, between fresh aspirations and the traditional spirit of race and religion. In this way he has altered and transposed the elements in the Biblical conflict, which is no longer between Deborah and Sisera, but between Deborah and Jael. The three actors in the drama stand out in relief like sculpture: Deborah, the prophetess who personifies the inflexible law, divine power, the will that can silence every feeling; Jael, the lover, at heart a timorous woman, convulsed and exalted by her passion; Sisera, the heroic general, with a heart that is pure and good, who desires to oppose the law of love to that which is enshrined in the divine commandment, and meets his doom; and beside these three integrated beings a fourth character with a complex spirit —the people, fickle and turbulent, now trembling with hatred and warlike fury, now dejected and tearful, an incoherent and elusive entity, formless material for heroes and leaders of men to mould.

When *Dèbora e Jaéle* was performed at the Scala Opera House in Milan on December 16th, 1922—the conductor was Arturo Toscanini, and the chief parts were played by Elvira Casazza, Giulia Tess and John Sample—there were those who said, or wrote, that Pizzetti's new opera was far more 'lyrical' than its predecessor and that the composer had repudiated or at any rate modified several of the fundamental principles of his theory. The reader will perceive that he had done neither of these things, for the very simple reason that he had never had any idea of abjuring lyrical composition in an absolute sense, and still less constructing a theory or system on which his operas were to have been modelled. I shall return to this second point, but meanwhile let me say at once, with reference to the first, that only when Pizzetti came to compose *Dèbora e Jaéle* did his ideal of musical drama find its complete realization from the point of view of rhythm and structure. As regards the concept of 'drama' and 'lyrical composition', there has sprung up in operatic terminology an ambiguity, not very different from that which exists in connection with the words 'classical' and 'romantic'. As a result the two terms are now regarded as expressing a complete antithesis, which holds good in every case and has gradually assumed the character of a criterion. Now I think that not only is it impossible to speak of lyrical composition and drama as two opposing and mutually exclusive concepts, but that it is not even established that the two αἰσθήσεις are always distinct and susceptible of differentiation. Pizzetti says that if opera is intended to express the life of the characters represented—and it could not be otherwise—it must take the form of drama. But life does not consist entirely of drama, just as it does not consist entirely of lyricism, or of action, or of the expression and conflict of passions. It also contains moments of contemplation, repose and serenity. The drama of life—drama in the widest sense of the word—is expressed in the very alternation, or rather simultaneity, of these and other phases, which can all be reduced to the common denominator represented by the person who lives through them. No lyrical phase is without elements of drama, and *vice versa*. The richness and, indeed, the meaning of a life consists in this very co-existence of different impulses and intonations, each of which helps to set off the others and enables us to appreciate them. The thought of Pizzetti, in so far as it makes drama the mainstay of opera, should accordingly be taken to imply that no lyrical oasis may or should interrupt the development of a drama, or cause any break in the continuity of the flow of feelings, or make us forget the rhythm that governs the course of life.[8] Lyricism and singing are therefore not ruled out, but both must be excluded if, says Pizzetti,[9] 'they do not arise and blossom forth with irresistible expansive force from the untying of a dramatic knot, from the surmounting of an emotional crisis, or from an uplifting of the spirit from the hostile reality of the world towards a higher consolation or beatitude'; if, let us add, they do not emerge spontaneously from the interplay of feelings in the form of momentary nuances or persistent undertones which, whether they be of primary or of secondary importance, always form an integral and necessary part of the whole. In short, Pizzetti—and this will help to clarify his attitude towards opera—does not rule out lyricism, but he cannot admit that drama should be subordinated to it: 'For five centuries—from the fourteenth to the nineteenth—composers of musical drama have persistently chosen to indulge in lyricism at all costs, and they have forced their characters to employ a purely lyrical mode of expression. Though there have of course, been certain exceptions, those who have sung, or in other words lived, in musical drama during the last five centuries have not been the characters. The words have been those of the authors, the melodies those of the composers.'[10]

These requirements are fulfilled by the musical drama *Dèbora e Jaéle*, and it is precisely because of this abundant vitality that it proves to be superior to *Fedra*. Not that we encounter here those redundant intermissions which Pizzetti roundly condemns in the Italian melodrama (especially in that of the eighteenth and the first half of the nineteenth centuries, which he regarded as 'the expression of a hedonistic art'), but drama and music are welded into a whole that transcends its parts, and, while the dramatic expression is liberated from the shackles of verbiage and tends to employ an ampler, freer medium, the lyrical expression is not unrestrainedly effusive, it does not assume autonomous

[8] Giuseppe Verdi did not say anything substantially different when he wrote to Ghislanzoni: 'Never fear, I do not mind *cabalette*, but I insist that they should have a subject and a justification . . . I am always of opinion that *cabalette* should be included when the situation demands.'

[9] *La Musica e il Dramma*, in *Rassegna Musicale*, January, 1932.

[10] *Ibid.*

Pizzetti at the time of 'Fedra', 1911

forms (strophe), and it is not unconcernedly and complacently self-contained. When Sisera is indulging at Jael's side in the sweet fulfilment of his amorous desire, and the music seems to slow down and cease as though suspended between heaven and earth, the drama is in reality not interrupted, for the moment of lyricism is necessitated by the character and not by the melody and its development. *Dèbora e Jaéle* contains several other passages of this kind, but there is no need to indicate them all. It is the characters that live and determine the musical expression: they each have their individual manner just as they each have their individual life. ('I have invented the entire life of every character,' Pizzetti wrote to me while he was creating the drama, 'so that they may resemble living beings; and some of their words actually refer to episodes that occurred during their past lives, before the period covered by the drama.') There is not a single personage in the whole of Pizzetti's work that is not strongly characterized by the composer, and differentiated by peculiarities of language, expression and intonation. As I have said, there are in *Dèbora e Jaéle* four main characters. Of these only the prophetess always shows us the same side of her nature, and reveals the same assurance. The other three—Jael, Sisera and the people—vary from scene to scene, and the last-named does so many times in a short space of time. But just as their psychological characteristics remain fundamentally unchanged, so too the æsthetic unity and coherence of each character is far more clearly perceptible in the varying form of the musical expression than it would be if there were a series of dominant themes.

Deborah's assurance is expressed in a uniform, solemn and prophetic style of speech, even when she grows excited and threatens the people or Jael with the wrath to come. When she appears, mid-way through the first act, the people are in an uproar. In the midst of the raging mob stands Jael, who has been accused of treason and sacrilege. Immediately the uproar dies down and changes to lamentation and prayer. Then Deborah speaks. Her words are accompanied by reiterated notes, short intervals, prolonged chords and sustained and ample phrases, in which we detect no tremor of doubt but rather the assurance of one who knows that truth is on her side, and in the midst of king of the Canaanites, Sisera, to go outside the walls of the city and join battle near the River Kishon. The contrast between the two could not be greater musically even though at this point Jael's will is completely dominated by that of the prophetess. Whenever Jael speaks her voice trembles with hope and faith, love and fear. As she did at her first appearance, and as she will always do afterwards, she expresses herself now in halting phrases, in bursts of melody that resemble cries or sobs, and in a voice that constantly falters. [See p. 35.]

When, in the last scene, Deborah and Jael meet face to face before the tent in which Sisera has fallen asleep, even the lover's heart has ceased to tremble. Passion and grief have transformed her, and in the presence of the inexorable prophetess she dares to lift her head and to proclaim aloud the new law. Hers is the victory, for she has found in love the reason for a higher life and a more vivid faith.

There is an affinity between Jael and the king of the Canaanites. The latter differs profoundly from his ferocious people, who are content with material pleasures. Pizzetti has represented him at the beginning of Act II among his princes and captains, alone with his thoughts and his desire, while around him the mob, like a wild beast, gives vent to its passions, uttering shrieks and blasphemies, telling tales of cruelties committed, and planning deeds of hatred and vengeance. The music with its strident theme:

at once tells us that we are in a very different world from that in which the first act ran its course. Sisera does not speak, and it seems 'that he does not even hear or see'. In fact, he is listening and inwardly seething with anger. When Japhia has completed the tale of his vile exploit his voice bursts forth like thunder, and he calls Adonizedec and bids him punish the miscreant. At once his figure commands attention, and his character—warlike, frank and loyal—is clearly delineated in the music. After the first imperious summons his declamation becomes forthright and resolute, but at the same time impassioned. One notices the difference in tone between the voice of Deborah, who derives fresh strength from something that is outside and above her, and that of Sisera, whose will is fortified by the passion that consumes him and by his desire to make his life complete. Sisera has been to Greece, whither he sailed in a Phoenician ship, and he has come back with his inner torment perhaps more acute. He has returned to his native shores hoping that he will be able to find in his kingdom the fulfilment of his heroic dream, and instead he has found himself surrounded by people so vulgar and barbarous that they repel him. This is what he tells us: 'No, not for this did I recross the sea/with steadfast eye fixed on the shining/Star of fire.' The same feeling of calm reconciliation to grief and the same grave, resolute accents are apparent in the first sentences that he utters when Jael, the woman he loves, comes before him with treachery in her heart: 'He alone is worthy to be exalted into the company of the eternal ones in heaven who can welcome death without in any way regretting life', and when, shortly afterwards, Jael attempts to kill him: 'If thou believest not that Sisera's life is a thousand times more precious than the lives of those who have sent thee from the shadows, and under cover thereof have set the trap for the lion which they dare not face, take thy sword and slay me, for I shall not be sorry to die.'

At first the hero awakens his amorous desire once more by objectifying it, as it were, in a serene and distant future, but little by little it is retransformed into a living reality. Indeed, it obtrudes itself upon him, raging within him like a burning torment, and the atmosphere of the music becomes ever more heated and impassioned. Idealism and sense, a yearning for life and a voluptuous preoccupation with death, are the two aspects of his passion which alternate and blend in his vibrant humanity.

37

But sense never degenerates into something oppressively physical; it is always redeemed by a lively consciousness of the ultimate good and the ultimate goal. Sisera, who has now been stripped of his pretensions, merely becoming a man confronted by the woman he loves, reveals the full measure of his goodness when, beaten and pursued by the Israelites, he takes refuge in Jael's tent. The words in which he addresses the lady have in them an element of timidity. He whispers them as though he were making a confession to himself, and in his final hour his beloved and his mother together form the subject of his thoughts. The purity of his filial devotion is not tainted by the sensuousness of his other love, and the same atmosphere pervades the two forms of the musical expression.

I have alluded to a fourth character in *Dèbora e Jaéle*—the Jewish people, who constitute the heterogeneous protagonist of a large part of Act I. (Naturally, those figures on which I have dwelt at length are not the only personages in the drama. Others —of secondary importance, but none the less necessary—are Azriel, Heber the Kenite, Japhia, the blind Enan, and Mara. And for each the composer has invented a characteristic tone and mode of expression.) Of Pizzetti's passion for choral work and of the wonderful passages that he offers us in this field I shall speak later. Here I shall content myself with drawing attention to the function and importance of the chorus as an element in the drama. The function of the chorus, which in *Fedra* was lyrical and static, becomes in *Dèbora e Jaéle* markedly dramatic and dynamic. Beginning from the conception of the chorus that obtained in Greek tragedy, Pizzetti has altered its function so as to make it conform to his æsthetic ideal of drama. Its new function is an active one, as anticipated—for reasons not entirely or exclusively of an artistic order—by Mazzini, who described it in the following passages in his *Filosofia della musica*:

Now why should not the collective individual known as the chorus acquire, like the people of which it is the natural mouthpiece, an independent, spontaneous existence? Why should it not constitute, in relation to the protagonist or protagonists, that element of contrast which is essential to any dramatic work? And in its subjective aspect, why should it not more often reflect, by the alternation and fusion of many interwoven and combined musical phrases, harmonized to form question and answer, the manifold variety of opinions, feelings, emotions and desires which normally seethe in the breasts of the multitude?

Pizzetti, while making use of earlier experience, has outmoded it by truly and completely freeing the chorus from all the bonds which held it in thrall to certain traditional forms and which in particular limited it to a restricted number of functions. He has made the mob speak and act with that changeableness and diversity of self-expression which is its most distinctive characteristic. He has set it in opposition now to the protagonists, now to itself, making it oscillate rapidly from an impulse tending in one direction to another having a contrary bias. But he has always succeeded in keeping it under control, reducing it at the fitting moment to a state of unity and unanimity. This is what he does in the first act of *Dèbora*, where he creates in the body of the chorus veritable 'levels' of musical perspective, which give the definite impression of a mob as it moves about, expressing its thoughts without any concern for musical architecture. For naturalness of expression and of development the whole of this expansive choral scene has no parallel in the field of opera save in the choral passages in the last act of *Boris*, where the people stand around the Boyar Kruchov uttering jeers and imprecations. Furthermore, in virtue of its emotive power and *élan*, I consider that this scene, together with the shorter one which brings the drama to a close, deserves to be mentioned in the same breath as some of the choruses of Verdi and Bellini (think of 'Guerra, guerra!' in *Norma*). That Pizzetti has made of the chorus not merely a part of the background but a real *dramatis persona* with a psychology of its own that is clearly defined and consistent—consistent, of course, in the sense that it obeys not the laws of logic but those of human experience—is confirmed by the fact that he has perceived intuitively and represented with incontestable clarity the entire course followed by the Israelitish mob in its evolution from the time when it was nothing but a formless mass of individuals awaiting someone who would control and rule it and impress his personality upon it so that it might develop a nature similar to its master's, until it assumed the character of a people and acquired a consciousness of itself and of its own strength. The appearance of Deborah, which is the point at which all the dramatic threads of the first act converge and meet, splits the act into two almost exactly equal parts. In the first the clamorous mob is subdivided into innumerable groups, all with different and variable proclivities. The second has as its theme the solemn formulation of a prayer and of the firm resolve to fight. In either case the mob is a living, active, dynamic and dramatic personage, like the individual characters, and perhaps more so than they.

From the observations so far made and from the examples of the musical language that have been quoted the reader will have understood that this language is not expressed in the form of recitative—using the word in its ordinary sense—nor in that of exuberant song. It is a well-known fact that opera-writers of the past, from Peri to Debussy, have, when faced with the problem of making their characters speak, adopted one of the following two expedients (of course, this is only a rough and unqualified classification, for every artist creates his own language, which differs from everyone else's). Either they have made them sing or they have made them declaim—or they have made them do both things successively in the same opera according to the circumstances. Thus we read in histories of music that the first opera or melodrama was declaimed and that later, at the end of the seventeenth and during the early years of the eighteenth centuries, the *melos* came more and more to take precedence over the drama and the individual parts definitely began to be sung. (There was, it is true, some *recitativo secco*; but this was so inexpressive and impersonal that it may, strictly, be regarded as a spoken and not a musical language.) And so we come across arias, *cabalette*, concerted arrangements and so forth. The nineteenth century witnessed little or no change, at any rate until about 1850. It is true that in the second half of the previous century there was Gluck, but his 'reform' did not attract many followers among opera-writers and his influence only revealed itself later, in Germany, with the advent first of Weber and then of Richard Wagner. In the second half of the nineteenth century the individual parts began once more to be declaimed, or at least there is apparent a sort of blending, or, if one prefers, contamination of the two styles—the lyrical and the dramatic—which still found new champions and opponents who oscillated between the two poles of attraction. As Debussy did before him in his unique and extremely individualistic *Pelléas*, Pizzetti has offered his own solution of the problem by turning his predecessors' experiments to account without, however, according any of them his unqualified approval. His vocal declamation is not the same as Gluck's recitative. Though full of grace, the latter is always characterized by a certain pompousness and solemnity which at times chills the fervour of its expression. It shows traces of its literary origin (let us not forget Calzabigi), and manifestly still owes something to the 'musical conversation' which was invented by the writer-composers (though they were writers rather than composers) of the *Camerata Fiorentina*, and which should be regarded more as a reaction and a pointer than as a definite step forward. Nor is it the same as Wagner's declamation —that 'melody of spoken verse' (*Wortversmelodie*) which, though its form is dependent on the raising and lowering of the tonic accent, is nevertheless too much bound up with the orchestration, of which it is at times merely a 'part'. Finally, it is not the same as Debussy's recitative, which conforms so strictly to the rhythm of the words and yet, by the very nature of Debussy's inspiration, is essentially lyrical, tending to create an atmosphere of repose and, if the expression is permissible, to surround the words with a suggestive air of vagueness and mystery; in which respect it is admirable in that it is utterly in keeping with the spirit of *Pelléas*.

One uses the word 'declamation' in connection with Pizzetti to distinguish this particular form of expression from pure song or lyrical amplification; for if the term did not constitute, seemingly at least, a paradox, one would say that Pizzetti's was a declamation in song-form. In reality what we are concerned with is a melodic organism having an intensely rhythmical quality, and characterized by the fact that, being inseparable from the words, it supports them, pervades their every syllable and enhances their emotional value. But the melody is not dictated by the words. Arising out of them, it combines with them to form a single entity. It does not destroy them or obscure them. On the contrary, it endues them with a meaning that it is beyond scope of verbal expression to convey. As one listens to the voices of Pizzetti's characters one seems to hear an unending melody, in which the words are all clearly perceptible and the music flows so naturally that it is impossible to say whether it originates

41

from the words or whether the reverse is not rather the case. The composer—the poet-composer—has intuitively conceived and reproduced the precise rhythmical pattern of every verse and phrase. He has made due allowance for all the pauses and for the original inflexions, scarcely failing to take account even of the refinements of tone and timbre that distinguish every word. It would accordingly be impossible to alter a note or to transpose an accent in a Pizzettian score without destroying, or at least reducing, its emotive power.

The trilogy of *Dèbora e Jaéle*, *Lo Straniero* and *Fra Gherardo*, which I will call the trilogy of the human creature's redemption through love (though there is certainly no idea of renunciation such as we find in *Parsifal*), was conceived in the artist's mind as a single entity. The original drafts of the dramas are traceable to the same period—1915 to 1921—and their common inspiration is apparent, both in the poems and in the scores. The essential traits of Sisera's character recur, with variations of emphasis, in the figures of the Stranger and Gherardo, just as the salient characteristics of Jael are reproduced in Maria and in Mariola. Though these personages find themselves in different environments, the members of each group all have the same life-style and react in the same way to different circumstances. Gherardo is still prompted by worldly motives, he is still subject to the pains and frailties of mortal flesh, alternately sinning and repenting and living in a world of egoism and hypocrisy, in which even the good are confounded and the wise grope blindly. The Pizzettian hero is not an ascetic and therefore does not tend to estrange himself from worldly life, spurning it as something diabolical. Rather does he wish to live it to the full, while comprehending its essence and its aims and welcoming everything in it that glorifies goodness, which is a gift from God, and humanity. He is a Christian demiurge, not a saint. Such a man is this Gherardo, who only occasionally sees the divine light. Only his passion and the fervour of his belief can redeem him. In an age of heresy and apostasy he is an artificer of fanatical creeds and of superstitions who has given all his possessions to the poor that he may follow the example of the Apostles. But one day by the wayside he meets a girl. Her name is Mariola, and she is a beautiful, humble creature. He is overpowered by love—a love that is still under the sway of unreasoning passion. Even before the first ecstasy of the lover has subsided, Gherardo ashamed of what he has done, abandons Mariola and goes far away with the Flagellant brotherhood. But he is destined to see Mariola once again. He encounters her at a decisive moment of his life—at the dawn of the day on which, in accordance with God's will, he is to lead the humble along the road to freedom. Mariola is now no longer beautiful, she is no longer capable of arousing his sensual desire. She is a mother who has lost her little one, the fruit of her love for Gherardo, against whom she has uttered no reproach. Now Gherardo understands the true meaning of his passion and desertion. 'In thy love God had sent me the surest of guides to lead me on my mortal journey among mankind...I was arrogant and base: I rejected life...And now...dreadful to relate...I am a father who has slain his child, and God will no longer have pity on me.' Through anguish and suffering he has fulfilled his destiny in the ways of love and truth. The Stranger, the nameless man who expiates his terrible crime of parricide and can now obtain grace only through the pure love of a sweet and amiable creature, is already conscious of his destiny. He has already heard the mysterious word of faith and hope. Henceforth he belongs to the world inhabited by those who have accepted life wholeheartedly, who are no longer rebellious but are strengthened by their acceptance of it. Hence his character is more clearly delineated than that of any other creature of Pizzetti's imagination. His spiritual ascent suffers no check. His whole story is stripped of embroidery, reduced to bare essentials, and uninterrupted by any digresssion. (Perhaps it is this simplicity, this complete absence of subsidiary episodes and lyrical interludes, that has suggested to some the idea that *Lo Straniero* adheres more strictly than Pizzetti's other operas to the principles embodied in his theory of the æsthetics of the drama.) To speak of progress in art is meaningless, as all are by now aware, and to speak of progress in connection with these dramas would be even more meaningless. But there is no doubt that in the Nameless One the characteristic traits of the Pizzettian hero seem to find more positive, concrete and representative expression. Against this purely imaginary background—according to the libretto the events take place 'in the time of the Shepherd Kings', but the indication is vague, nor does the text seem to relate the action to a particular moment in the history of human society—Pizzetti has been able to put into the mouths of the Stranger and Maria all the sentiments with which he is familiar, to express them in the forms that he prefers, and to clothe them in those emotions through which alone, in his opinion, life acquires spiritual reality. At the end of the first act, the second part of which has been intensely dramatic, its tranquillity being disturbed by conflicting passions, when the Stranger is preparing to resume his journey 'alone with his heart and with Him Who knows every road', an old man utters the following words, which all repeat with him: 'The world is wide, and beneath the vast heavens there are so many lands and oceans, so many races, that the day is too short for man to learn everything. But the human heart is a great and fathomless abyss, whereat he is affrighted. God alone enters within it and reads its thoughts—the God Who knows every beginning and judges every end!' And we hear a solemn chorus, in which little by little the voices of all the characters join, and which seems to cease almost completely as soon as it begins. A powerful atmosphere of peace and eternity is created by the fusion of orchestra and voices—an atmosphere partly of this world, partly of the next. These words of peace seem to me to constitute so clearly, within the framework of this opera, a moral 'absolute' that I for my part have always thought they would form an appropriate description of Pizzetti's ideals.

Lo Straniero, which was first performed at the Royal Opera House in Rome on April 29th, 1930,[11] was written between 1922 and 1925, that is before *Fra Gherardo*. The composition of the latter took place between September 1925, and September 1927, but it preceded *Lo Straniero* in order of presentation. It was first performed at the Scala Opera House, Milan, on May 16th, 1928, Arturo Toscanini conducting and the leading roles being taken by Florica Cristoforeanu and Antonio Trantoul. The musical affinities between *Lo Straniero* and *Débora e Jaéle* are more pronounced than those between the latter and *Fra Gherardo*.

[11] The conductor was Gino Marinuzzi, and the chief parts were played by Maria Zamboni, Renato Zanelli, Giacomo Vagli and Gaetano Viviani.

More than once King Hanòch speaks in tones reminiscent of the prophetess, and the atmosphere in which the conversation between the Nameless One and Maria develops brings to memory that of the closing scenes in *Dèbora*. The Stranger is condemned to resume his journey through the desert, and he must set out before dawn. But the king's daughter, the gentle Maria, wishes to go with him. She realizes that in his company alone will she feel that she is alive, and she is ready to face every kind of danger and suffering. Such an air of sweetness emanates from the music in this scene that the sadness of the hour is forgotten. In Maria, this Christian Antigone, we see exalted the loftiest womanly virtues, all of which spring from the heart in the form of pure emotions. The climax of the action is now

expressed in the singing. Only a lyrical catharsis can untie the knot of pain; and the desire of the man who does not fear death becomes the ultimate and most perfect reality that his spirit knows, namely Grace. [See p. 45.]

Just as *Lo Straniero* has a single theme, the essence of the drama being concentrated in its ending, so *Fra Gherardo* is rich in episodic motifs and picturesque passages. In technique and structure the former is akin to Greek tragedy, the latter to the mediæval mystery. As in classical tragedy, so in *Lo Straniero*, antecedent events are not represented on the stage but described at second hand, while in *Fra Gherardo* different incidents are revealed as it were on a vast fresco. We see portrayed cathedrals and palaces, the people and the aristocracy, monks and bishops, and our attention is attracted by each of these persons and things in turn. *Lo Straniero* rigorously observes the three classical unities of action, time and place—the plot unfolds without interruption between sunset and dawn, and the scene is identical in the first and second acts—whereas nine years elapse between the first two acts of *Fra Gherardo* and the scene varies from one act to the next.

The tragedy of Gherardo is wholly invented, but he was a historical character, and Friar Salimbene has described him, though differently from Pizzetti, in his *Cronaca*. He has also described the band of fanatics who followed him, the army of the Apostolics, that 'army of stupid, despicable scoundrels and swineherds' who busied themselves with their work of guiding men by precept and example in the region of Parma, about the year 1260. The composer has scrupulously primed himself with documents relating to this period, but as in the earlier case of *Dèbora*, he has not allowed his erudition to obscure the human drama. He has tried to get right into the mind of the fanatical crusader, to understand the impulses behind his actions and the causes of what ultimately befalls him. Although, as has been said, the episodic element is rich and varied, it does not impede the rhythm of the main action, and all the limelight is concentrated on the two figures of Gherardo and Mariola. The charm of the countryside and the suggestive power of his own landscape, of which Pizzetti has always been conscious and which he has often expressed in his compositions, have not distracted his attention from the inner nucleus of the drama. This has constituted the focal point of his psychological inquiry, and even in nature he has always seen the reflection of man.

As I have said, the musical content is not unlike that of the earlier operas. Nevertheless, it tends to be more compactly arranged, being concentrated around clearly distinguished and recurrent groups of themes. It is noticeable that lyrical episodes occur more frequently in *Fra Gherardo* than in the other operas—they are nearly always identifiable with the figure of Mariola —and we find taking shape, almost imperceptibly, self-contained musical entities, strophic in character. Examples are the passage in Act I where in his mind's eye Gherardo sees Mariola's mother offering her little one to the Lord; the Provençal ballad which comes immediately after the tender Gospel episode of Mary Magdalene; the symphonic interlude between the scenes, which is wholly and exuberantly vocal; the Flagellant's hymn of praise in Act II; the whole of the duet between Gherardo and his lady; and the finale of the opera, which is concerned with the death of Mariola. A more incisive group of themes, adapted to the various characters and to the basic sentiments which motivate the plot, governs the symphonic evolution of the opera and transforms the orchestration into a network of counterpoint which, though it is more finely-wrought than is the case in the earlier works, is always sensitive to the nuances of the drama and modifiable

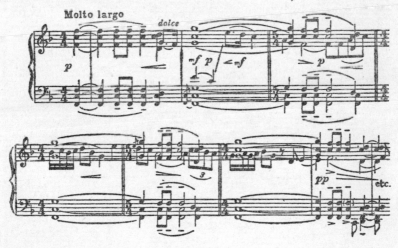

accordingly. A fundamentally important part in the development of the opera is played by themes like the twofold one which occurs at the beginning [see p. 47]; or this one, which is among the most lyrical and impassioned themes that Pizzetti has created, and which might be called the love-theme:

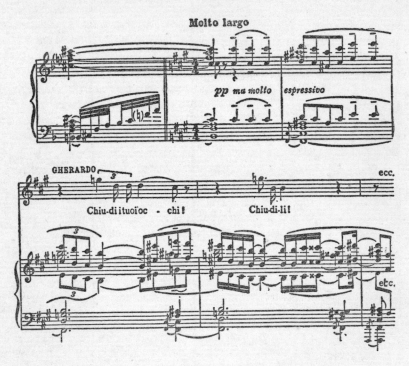

or the plaintive one that we find in Act II, expressing the weariness and suffering of the oppressed people:

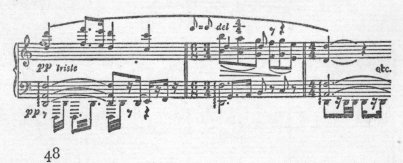

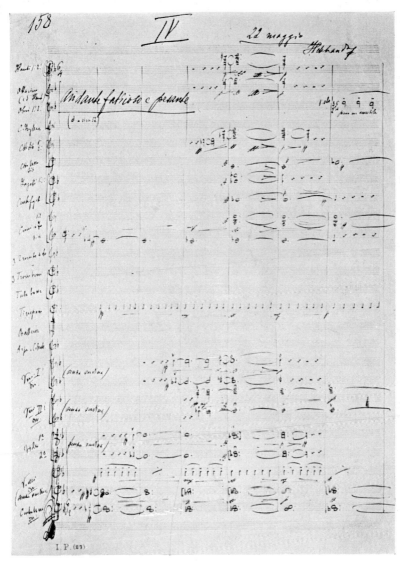

A page from the autograph of
Symphony in A

This last theme is developed in the first scene of Act III, together with the rhythmic motif of the rebellious people. The whole of this act is a polyphonic fresco of a breadth and pathos with few parallels in the history of opera. Gherardo, who has been accused of heresy, is led to the funeral-pyre that has been erected in front of Parma Cathedral. The mob fill the square and press against the armed guard in an effort to free the man who promised to raise them up, and will now, in the presence of the Judges, confess that he has sinned 'against life and against God', that he has offended Christ, and that he has preached a doctrine of hatred. In order to save Mariola he has performed an act of shame, but he now has a clearer conception than ever of the ideal law which governs his life. Mariola, who has been struck by a townswoman, dies and Gherardo starts to walk to the funeral-pyre. The people, who a moment before were showering curses on the traitor, fall on their knees as the sacrifice begins. Through the black, low-hanging clouds there suddenly appears a ray of sunshine.

The background of *Orsèolo*, which was performed at the 1935 *Maggio Musicale Fiorentino*, is Venice—not as it was in the glittering period of the Republic, nor even during the decadence of the eighteenth century, but the Venice of the period which followed the war in Candia and Morea and which marks the beginning of the crisis. The rise of the new 'democratic' state and the resulting conflict—political, social and emotional—due to the last desperate defence put up by the aristocrats, constitute the fundamental idea of the opera. From the drama of this moment in history, with its repression, its gloom and its sorrow, there emerges the drama of a few men, epitomized in the clash of two wills, equal in strength and resolved on a fight to the finish. In the contrast between the old senator Marco Orsèolo, in whose veins runs the blood of doges and *condottieri*, and the young Rinieri Fusinèr, who can boast of nothing but his spiritual integrity and purity and his right to live, lies the key to the story, which is so dominated by passion that at times it becomes almost inhuman. Between the two men there stands the gentle figure of a woman, Contarina, Orsèolo's daughter, who can entertain only good thoughts, is incapable of hatred, and wishes to encompass the triumph of feelings of peace and love over all

D

animosities of party. She is an exquisitely Pizzettian creature, closely akin to those we encountered in the earlier dramas.

But if the Contarina with whom we are confronted is endowed with the same characteristics as her elder sisters (Maria and Mariola), the dominant theme of the drama is at variance with the Pizzettian ethic as expressed in his greatest works, and I do not think we can assert that the author has derived any advantage from building his story around this Venetian King Lear, who is prompted by pride rather than love, and is at times positively inhuman in his determination. The drama is somewhat gloomy and monotonous. Even the music bears some slight traces of this mood; I would say that, except in a few scenes, it is rather lacking in freedom of expression. Compared with the earlier operas *Orsèolo* is a psychological drama. This, perhaps, is why the author has felt it necessary to insert in the first and third acts, by way of interludes, two large-scale choral scenes of an objective character. In the first, which takes place at night on the Riva degli Schiavoni, a masquerade passes through the crowd that is waiting to bid farewell to the Venetian soldiers as they set sail for the East. It is easy to appreciate that the gaiety of the scene is somewhat artificial, and that the contrast between the thoughtlessness of the actors in the masque and the air of pathos which surrounds the departing troops creates a dramatic situation that is bound to be effective. The second interlude also has the Riva degli Schiavoni for a background, but this time it is a bright, calm morning. Victory has smiled on the Venetians and the people are acclaiming the returning warriors, having formed a procession led by the Doge. Scenes from everyday life are interspersed with outbursts of exultation. The stage is filled with knots of people, arguing or playing cards, until the arrival of the procession. Here we have one of the finest choral passages that Pizzetti has written. It recalls the chorus of the Flagellants in *Fra Gherardo* and that of the Catechumens in *La Nave*. [See p. 51.]

The words of the song are taken from a genuine Venetian hymn of the period—'O Venice, Queen of the Sea,/blessed standard-bearer of Christ,/raise aloft thy glorious head,/crowned with laurel-wreaths and roses.' As regards the musical language of *Orsèolo*, if we compare it with that of the earlier operas, there is

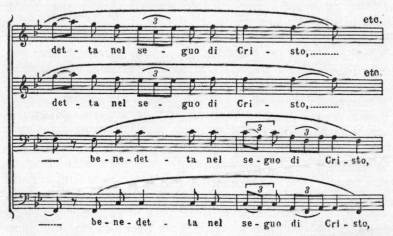

nothing new to note apart from a tendency on the part of the composer to confine himself even more strictly to declamation and *arioso*. Some might discern in this tendency signs of the influence of Verdi—the Verdi of *Simon Boccanegra* and *Otello*.

L'Oro, a drama in three acts, written between 1938 and 1942, should have been performed in Florence during the following year. On account of the war, however, it was only introduced to the public in 1947. It was presented at the Scala, Milan, in February of that year, and at the Rome Opera House a few weeks later, the author conducting. *L'Oro* reveals signs of the acute crisis which at that time faced all Italian artists—victims of a mad folly that was to bring so much sorrow to their country— more especially in that it embodies social as well as moral motifs, on which Pizzetti lays even more stress than in his earlier operas. The most important point is that in *L'Oro* we no longer have a 'costume' play. What I mean is that, although the period is indefinite,[12] we feel, as has been shrewdly appreciated by the critic Gavazzeni,[13] that the indication *today* should be especially stressed because of the grim topicality of a theme that has persisted in human affairs ever since the first fratricide. In this recent and most important work Pizzetti characterizes gold, and the conflicts of material interests to which gold gives rise, as the chief cause of the evils that beset all ages, and therefore also our own. On the plateau of Carpineta, which is the scene of the action, there has grown up a community of men who freely acknowledge as their leader Giovanni de' Neri. At a certain stage the discovery of a vein of gold inspires them with the idea of rebelling against their Leader, whose crime is that he has not revealed where the treasure is hidden nor allowed his people to have a share in it. But Cristina, Giovanni's wise and far-sighted spouse prefers to sacrifice her young life and bury the gold for ever in the bowels of the earth, sure as she is that its acquisition would only bring sorrow to all. Her death is destined to inaugurate a new era in the lives of the people, who, having abandoned all their dreams of a sudden access of wealth, will have to return to the land, to work, and to the serenity of family life. We are confronted with concepts and problems which had already been treated by other dramatists in the past. Pizzetti has examined them afresh, dealing with them from a topical angle without, however, introducing political elements of recent origin. But however interesting and pertinent these problems may be, they would not constitute adequate material for the kind of drama that is an indispensable foundation for opera did not the human aspect, the personal feelings of the principal characters, enter into, or rather dominate, their treatment. Pizzetti had this in

[12] The author writes: 'The scene is the plateau of Carpineta. The action takes place today, or yesterday, or in an even more distant and indefinite past.'

[13] G. Gavazzeni, '*L'Oro*' *di I. Pizzetti—Guida Musicale*, Milan, 1946 (p. 57).

mind when he endowed Cristina with the qualities of a timorous, tender woman, one who is first and foremost a wife and mother, lacking the understanding needed for the solution of problems but possessing instead that feminine intuition which suggests a solution even before the precise terms of the problem have been formulated. The victory is with Cristina, who is incapable of excessively gradiose dreams and whose ambitions do not extend beyond the limits of her own family circle—her husband, and a child who has been deaf from birth and will only acquire the gift of speech when he sees his mother on her deathbed.

In *L'Oro* the choral element becomes once more of first importance; nowhere in the rest of the opera is the music of such undoubted quality. Adequate evidence of this is provided by the lengthy choral passage which we find at the very beginning of Act I—a passage whose polyphonic structure takes us back to the scene in the first act of *Dèbora e Jaéle* which is in certain respects analogous in spirit. Here too the treatment of the piece is essentially dramatic: witness the many breaks and interruptions, the sudden cries and exclamations which reflect the psychological make-up of the individual characters. It is, so to say, one of those scenes which, in an opera by a nineteenth-century composer, would have been the cue for a final concertato. Here, however, it marks not an ending but rather the establishment of a situation which is destined to develop in the ensuing scenes of the opera. A theme of particular importance, the appearance of which in the score will often have definitive significance, is that associated with Giovanni, Leader of the Community. I reproduce it herewith, observing that in virtue of the flexibility and incisiveness of its design I regard it as one of the most 'Pizzettian' themes in the opera.

Pizzetti's most recent opera, *Vanna Lupa*, reverts in more than one respect to the style of his earliest pieces (such as *Débora* and *Fra Gherardo*), particularly as regards its comparative lack of rhetoric and its power of synthesis.

His decision to write an opera with a Florentine setting dates back about seven years. 'During a short stay in Florence, following an absence of several years,' says Pizzetti, 'I went one evening to the Piazza della Signoria. As I looked at the Palazzo dei Priori I suddenly saw before me, in imagination, the final scene of *Vanna Lupa*. It was so vivid, so detailed, that even if I had so desired I could not have rid myself of the feeling that I must write an opera which culminated in that scene.'

The author was kept occupied for a year with the studies that preceded the drafting of the text of the poem, whose action he chose to ascribe to the second half of the fourteenth century, because (he says) that was the most dramatic and the most unequivocally Florentine epoch in the whole of Florence's history. He made a study, supplemented by copious notes, of histories and ancient chronicles, including Machiavelli's *Storia*, the *Cronache* of Giovanni and Matteo Villani, and the annals of Velluti. He also read some valuable fourteenth-century chronicles, such as those of Ser Nofri and Ser Piero delle Riformazioni and of Marchionne di Coppo Stefani, and Squittinatore's Diary; these were suggested by the comparatively recent historical works of Gino Capponi, Emiliani Giudici and Giuseppe Odoardo Corazzini. Between the commencement of the first draft of the libretto and the simultaneous notation of the musical themes on the one hand, and the completion of the third and final draft and the score on the other,[14] there elapsed five fruitful years (1942 to the end of 1947).

The action of *Vanna Lupa* takes place between a Saturday and a Monday in the May of an unspecified year between 1343, when the Duke of Athens was expelled, and 1379, *i.e.* during that period of Florentine history which was marked by political and social unrest and strife culminating in the rebellion of the Ciompi. It is therefore essential that the *dramatis personae* should reflect in their make-up and meaning not only their individualities but also the various social classes which they represent and the

[14] Pizzetti writes his theatrical and symphonic works directly in full score.

general sentiments proper to contemporary society. The latter is also actively personified in the chorus, which at one moment is divided into opposing factions, at another united by common sentiments of humanity.

Although the heroine of the drama bears the name of a glorious and extremely powerful Aretine family of the period (she is called Vanna dei Tarlati—the name Lupa is a sobriquet—and is the widow of one Ricci, a Florentine, who has been killed by political enemies), and although names of ancient Florentine families are assigned to other characters,[15] none of Pizzetti's *dramatis personae* is taken from history. Like the events depicted, they are wholly figments of the author's imagination.

As regards the musical conception of the drama, I have nothing to add to what I have written of its predecessors. Here too the vocal expression develops in an unbroken stream; it is fully apparent and comprehensible, and never stagnates in pools of lyrical song. It is a kind of melodious declamation, following the accents of the words and sentences with simple, smooth interludes, which often broaden into short interpolations in the traditional style of opera. Perhaps in *Vanna Lupa* we encounter with greater frequency those echoes of Verdian *arie*, in which, I again repeat, we discern the obscure, primal origins of Pizzetti's vocal expression. But we seem to discern besides in this most recent opera a definite tendency to simplify and clarify the orchestration, and hence to invest the movement of the drama with greater vigour and flexibility. This is particularly the case in the scene in the second act between Vanna Lupa and Ririna, which ends on a singularly moving episode with the mother expressing the grief which up to now she has held in check. Needless to say, the choral passages, which are numerous and extensive, are worthy to stand beside the best in Pizzetti.

While on the subject of the dramas I may mention those other pieces by Pizzetti which a rough definition would classify under the heading of 'Incidental music'. (I associate the two groups, however, more on account of their external similarities than because there is a basic affinity between them.) This is a *genre*

---

[15] E.g. Vieri dei Ricci, Vanna's son, and Lapo Velluti, step-father of Caterina, who is betrothed to Vieri. There are also characters named Pazzi, Strozzi, Alemanni, *etc.*

which has illustrious antecedents in the history of music, having been cultivated by composers ranging from Schumann (*Manfred*) to Mendelssohn (*A Midsummer Night's Dream*), from Grieg to Debussy (but the oldest and most renowned examples are still those afforded by Greek tragedy and the mediæval liturgical drama). It enjoyed a great vogue during the last century, especially in Germany and England. Modern producers in those countries, which awoke long before Italy to the importance of the musical element in drama, have always sought the collaboration of composers. There have been no plays of any importance for which such impresarios as Reinhardt and Copeau, to mention two eminent examples, have not envisaged and sponsored musical accompaniments. An initial essay in this kind of collaboration was furnished by Pizzetti in the music for *La Nave*. But we cannot, strictly speaking, describe this as incidental music because the greater, and undoubtedly the best, part of it consists of choral work and not of illustrations of the drama. It should therefore be considered separately; and I shall accordingly discuss it later on.

When, on the other hand, we come to examine *La Pisanella* we find that the collaboration is closer and more purposeful. Here we no longer have choruses but orchestral music—eleven symphonic pieces, interludes and dances, embracing the whole of d'Annunzio's poem—and in addition a number of interpolations during the course of the dialogue (for instance, the scene between the king and the beggar, at the end of the prologue). Yet the effect of this closer collaboration is not to add in any real sense to the power of the drama, or to illuminate the words, or to throw the figurative expression into greater relief. As to 'melology', *i.e.* the use of music to emphasize speech—the παρακαταλογή of the Greeks—Pizzetti had condemned it even before he wrote *La Pisanella*[16] in an essay dealing with Mendelssohn's music for the *Antigone* of Sophocles and the general problem of the modern presentation of Greek tragedy, which he desired to see performed either without any music at all or as grand opera—'interpreted by the characters through the medium of song, and by the orchestra in the language of symphony', in other words translated into musical drama.

'In my opinion,' he wrote in the article cited below, "melo-

[16]In the journal *Il Momento*, Turin, 1910.

logy" is a misguided form of art; for the contrast between the imprecise intonation of the spoken word, which, however rich and varied in shade it may be, is monochromatic, and the precise and polychromatic intonation of orchestral music is so great that it is impossible for the one to be effectively implemented and reinforced by the other. All the experiments in "melology" carried out during the last century, and even the most recent essays in this field, seem to me to be the result of a lamentable deviation from æsthetic standards, though I recognize that some music of this kind has great expressive power in itself...'

For the rest, although the composer endeavoured to fall into line with the poet, critics noted their fundamental disparity of outlook and æsthetic intention. As I have said already, in *Fedra* Pizzetti had succeeded in rendering this less apparent, minimizing the handicap which resulted from the fact that the drama exercised an absolute, imperious tyranny over the composition of the music. A certain effort to exteriorize the expression and to heighten its pictorial quality is to be noted in the score of *La Pisanella*. For sonority of orchestration, gracefulness of melody and brilliance of harmony this is perhaps the composer's most 'd'Annunzian' opera, the one in which the richness and variety of the images seem to drown the inner voice of the music. The passionate orientalism of d'Annunzio's poem has led, and sometimes driven, Pizzetti—if only for brief moments—to indulge in an excess of colour and in a number of lyrical effusions which seem to have evaded his strict control. Even in passages like the *Danza dell'amore e della morte profumata*, which is as compact and vibrant as a powerful dramatic perspective, we find examples of this vivid embroidery which in my opinion reflect moments of creative weariness. But the spirit of Pizzetti breathes in the finest pages of the score and makes them quite independent of the poem. We may even consider that the latter does not exist save as a succession of motifs to be exploited by the composer. My instinctive predilections are for those passages from which the merest suspicion of ornamentalism is absent, those in which there is a minimum of gesture and movement and which are least trammelled by dramatic considerations without on that account having less internal movement and dramatic power. I prefer the prelude to Act III, which is based on the two most expressive and important themes in the opera—the obscure and tortuous theme associated with the 'pitiless' Queen,

and what may be termed the 'rose theme', since it is fully developed in the last dance.

This theme is lucid, animated and pliant; and in the final bars of the prelude, to the liquid, sonorous strains of flutes and clarinets, it becomes even smoother and lighter. I prefer too the saraband for strings alone, which bears the title *La Danse de Pauvreté et de parfait Amour, autrement dite la Danse basse de l'Épervier*. This piece has by now become a part of the repertory of symphony orchestras. The rhythm and outlines of the music here express the most intense passion, rendered in the purest classical form.

Even the music composed for the *Sacra Rappresentazione di Abram e d'Isaac*, despite its closer adherence to the spirit of the subject, cannot be regarded as a homogeneous work of art. It should rather be looked upon as a series of lyrical fragments; even

now that Pizzetti has written a new score in which the whole of
Feo Belcari's poem is set to music in order to eliminate the disparity between words and accompaniment, the unpleasing
effects of which he demonstrates in the article referred to. The
original fault of this work is still apparent, namely its lack of a
clearly defined musical rhythm and a genuine dramatic structure. At one moment the music reveals a lyrical abandon which
suggests that it has shaken off the burden of the words: at another,
it becomes merely a synthesis of sound, a superfluity. The composer leaves the poet in possession of the field, and since in the
present instance the latter does not always succeed in investing
his images, which are an intuition of his piety and his faith rather
than a creation of his fancy, with intense dramatic life, the
emotional temperature is lowered in those very passages which
should be marked by greater tension—for example, in the scene
that depicts the sacrifice of Isaac. Except in the cases that I have
indicated, the music of *Abramo e Isacco* is less superficial than that
of *La Pisanella*, and almost the whole of its inspiration is lyrical
and frankly religious. The finest passages are those at the beginning of the *Rappresentazione* which foreshadow *Dèbora*, with their
slow, sweet theme for horns and trumpets; the whole of the
proclamation of the feast-day, which for all its priestly calm is
already instinct with human emotion; the instrumental music
which coincides with the departure of Abraham and Isaac for
the sacrificial mountain; the grand chorus which echoes the
words of the Angel and stays Abraham's hand—here the scene
is expressed in music of truly heavenly tenderness:

—and finally the lament of Sarah and her handmaids, as an accompaniment to which Pizzetti has included in his later version a piece of recitative that is full of nobility and fervour.

Perhaps because its text is one of those which have no independent existence but only come to life on the stage, the score of the *Rappresentazione di Santa Uliva*, which was written in little more than a month during the spring of 1933, demonstrates far more convincingly than the one that we were discussing a moment ago, the importance of music's part in spoken drama. No one who has seen this play can believe any longer in the possibility of presenting that most moving story on the stage without the music. Here the music and the production have indeed contributed to the creation of a work of art; and a rare unity of purpose on the part of the composer and the producer (Jacques Copeau) has yielded superb results. The kind of spectacle that was staged in the Great Cloister of Santa Croce in Florence was conceived in a moment of grace and will not easily be forgotten. The unknown sixteenth-century author has found in Pizzetti a kindred spirit. The composer has sensed the meaning of his naive expressions not with the understanding of a man of letters but with the soul of a poet, and the musical stylization of the feelings and attitudes of Uliva and the other figures in her story has produced a fresh and living imaginative work. The 'subjects' of Pizzetti's music comprise a hunt, a battle, a scene in an inn, the symbolization of a heartbreaking journey amid the changing seasons, a coronation, a wedding, etc.; but, as with the primitives, the 'subject' is merely a vehicle for the expression of love, faith, and humility in the face of divine things and those human things which emanate from God. Hence the illustrative elements in these scenes are never in the foreground and are always sensed intuitively through the medium of the sentiment which controls the actions of the heroine. An external episode becomes an inward transformation, a change of colour, a shudder of emotion, or a mental process. An excellent example of this transference of the visual to an emotional plane is furnished by the *pièce de résistance* of the score—Uliva's journey in quest of her child who has been stolen from her by the Evil One. It is a heartbreaking odyssey, punctuated by sudden hopes and tragic disappointments until she finds him again in the mystical light of the

Empyrean. A single theme is heard while Uliva is on her journey, a lowly theme which seems as though it is striving to express the arduousness of her climb towards the light that eludes her and the yielding of her sorrowful spirit:

It is a theme of rare excellence and beauty that retires from individual expression, but conforms so finely to the character of the protagonist that we do not wish for any variations or innovations or other elaborative *tours de force*. The music awakens the deepest echoes of an ideal past—an indefinable past that is like the legendary childhood of the world, when the Virgin and her Divine Son appeared to the faithful and guided their footsteps, and the Evil One assumed the symbolic guise of a high-born but hard-hearted man, and the wings of the angels diffused a shimmering radiance betwixt heaven and earth. Among all the musical works of our time that are termed sacred and have as their purpose the exaltation of God in His glory it may be asserted that few are more 'religious' than this tribute to St Olive, while none constitutes a more worthy accompaniment to the portrayal of the Miracle.

CHAPTER III

The Choral Music

THE BOOK WHICH Giovanni Tebaldini has written on Pizzetti testifies to his affection for the man who was once his pupil at the Musical Academy.[17] The author makes frequent references to the singular fervour with which the young composer studied the most characteristic forms of vocal expression—songs for solo voice as well as for several, the *genres* examined ranging from the Gregorian to the early seventeenth-century part-song (in which there were already signs of the baroque), so that the evolution of the motet and the madrigal also came under review. The only compositions of those remote years which their author considered not undeserving of publication were three choral pieces: an *Ave Maria* for three voices with organ, referred to as Opus 1, a responsory for Good Friday (*Tenebrae factae sunt*, for six different voices), and a *Tantum ergo* for three male voices with organ accompaniment. Pizzetti's preference for songs, more especially part-songs, was dictated by a compulsive spiritual urge, which became steadily more pronounced and imperious, and by influences from folk-song, especially choral folk-song, so frequently heard in his own Emilia. He had an innate feeling that life should be lived religiously, in the widest meaning of the term, and that mankind formed a brotherhood to which it should be the aim of all activity to give expression: he felt that nature was not inanimate and indifferent to the creature, but alive with a thousand kindred voices. Such feelings moved him to express himself in such a way that all these

[17] Giovanni Tebaldini, *Ildebrando Pizzetti nelle 'Memorie'*, Fresching, Parma, 1931.

62

voices should be heard in a multiplicity of sound that issued forth from a single essence. It must have seemed to the young composer that the way to live more intensely, to turn to account and multiply a hundredfold his powers as a man and as an artist, was to cultivate a sense of oneness with all who love their fellow creatures and to sing with them of joy and suffering, life and death. It is in this, even more than in a more strictly musical sense, that we must understand the conception of vocality to which Pizzetti has often referred when speaking of his own works and those of others. Indeed, apropos the music of Bellini he has written: 'Vocalization or song is, in short, a wholly subjective quality of musical expression. It is emotion, humanity and hence, by implication, essential . . . The beauty of pure song—of song that is truly vocal—lies in its spirit and *raison d'être*. It is a beauty that one feels . . .' Pizzetti's conception, then, does not establish any artistic 'hierarchy', but, as we have already seen in our discussion of his conception of drama, its breadth and profundity are increased until music and vocalization are identified, so that it affords a debatable but lucid criterion for the appraisal of musical works of art.

The study of the great models of classical polyphony made Pizzetti conscious, then, of the infinite wealth of modes of expression of which vocal counterpoint was a potential source, and of the shameful decadence of the Italian composers who had completely forgotten those wonderful pieces or regarded them as mere historical curios. A long time had elapsed since the day when Guiseppe Verdi had launched his appeal for the creation of an Italian vocal quartet,[18] and only in the course of those years did Tebaldini, having been appointed director of the Parma Musical Academy in 1897, break down an unprecedented barrier of hostility and distrust (of which he tells us himself in the above-mentioned work) and reveal to his pupils the unsuspected treasure that was enshrined in the works of Palestrina, Marenzio, Lasso, Vittoria, Gesualdo and Monteverdi. The variety and abandon of these pieces must have been a source of joyful wonderment to a young man like Pizzetti, who had thought until then that choral work was exclusively associated with the academic exercises of a few isolated composers of

[18] In a letter to O. Arrivabene dated March 30th, 1879.

so-called religious or liturgical music, with the lucubrations of learned research-workers, or at the most generous estimate with the training of students of counterpoint. For such was the state of affairs as regards choral music in Italy, and it had prevailed for some time. (Unfortunately, moreover, if we ignore a few special cases and some occasional glimmerings of revival, it is not very different even today.) Pizzetti continued to study the above-named masters with great diligence for many years—we have reason to believe that Gesualdo was one of those who attracted him most, in virtue of the highly dramatic tendencies of his madrigals—nor, as may well be imagined, did he cease to do so after he had gained his diploma. But if his labours were prolonged and diligent, they were not rendered sterile by a preoccupation with questions of doctrine, nor was their fervour diminished by any obsession with technicalities. As in the case of Greek music and the Gregorian chant, which he likewise subjected to intensive contemplation, the viewpoint from which Pizzetti considered the works of these masters was always that of the artist, never that of the scholar. Nor, in order to follow a fashion, did he turn to the past, hoping to find in it convenient suggestions and motifs which he could transplant bodily into modern settings. The case of the Gregorian must suffice as an example. In the whole of Pizzetti's work there are hardly any specifically Gregorian themes or genuinely liturgical melodies: they may be counted on the fingers of one hand, and they all occur in the early works. Yet the influence which those ancient modes exerted on the structure of Pizzetti's melodies may be sensed, if not seen, in the whole of his work, like a subtle perfume. It is particularly apparent in *Dèbora* and *Lo Straniero*.[19] It is the artist's style that has evolved under the influence of this music: he has felt its purity and its loftiness. But he has lived through and re-created everything for himself. In the critical hour of modern tonality Pizzetti has tried to prevent the disappearance of tonal sensibility, which he has based on the modal principle of ecclesiastical music. But he has avoided all ambiguity and incoherence, together with any suggestion of artifice. We find in his work an approach similar to that of certain composers to folk-song.

[19] Note in the two final movements of the last-named work the echoes of the doxological melismata and of the Easter hymns of exultation.

Stage Design for Act III 'Fra Gherardo'
Scala, Milan, 1928

Whereas the latter has been completely assimilated in the work of such composers as Béla Bartók and the later de Falla, in Dvořák, or, nearer our own time, Sinigaglia, it is like a heterogeneous inert substance that remains floating on the surface of the pure essence of another metal, *i.e.* the Brahmsian style of the two artists in question.

The first work in which we find Pizzetti's stylistic personality expressed is the group of pieces composed between 1905 and 1907 for d'Annunzio's *La Nave*. With one exception these pieces are choral and, apart from the *Inno a Diona*, religious, or rather liturgical. What melodies has the composer employed? He himself tells us:[20]

Accordingly, I wrote the melodies of *La Nave* in the forgotten 'modes' of primitive liturgical music, which is the same as saying that I wrote them in the modes of Greco-Latin music. When I came to compose the melody for each chorus I selected the 'mode' which corresponded most exactly in character to the meaning and expression of the text of the poem. I did not choose to regard this character as being fixed by the definition which ancient Greek or Latin theorists, philosophers or the first musicologists of the Church had prescribed, but preferred to cultivate a personal sense of it deep down in my own being. Sometimes it has happened that a given 'mode' has acquired in my music a richer and more varied expressive character, one that in not a few cases has been far from corresponding to the definition offered by this or that ancient writer. This has been due to the polyphony, which, by showing up the musical theme in a different light and redistributing the shadows, has emphasized one of the expressive characteristics of the mode or has reduced its force.

Thus, as I have said, the melodies—apart from those of the *Ave Maris Stella*—were all invented by the composer, even if some of them were evolved from ancient νόμος (as formulated in the *Tonarius* of Reginone di Prun) by a method which demonstrates how Pizzetti has been able to translate into the modern notation the melodic richness of the original νόμος. Here is an example of this method [see page 66].

But his polyphonic composition already reveals that freedom and sureness in handling the parts and assigning an expressive function to each of them which all esteem so highly in his choral work. This composition is never overloaded or congested: on the contrary, it is light and pellucid. But every part has an existence

[20] In *Rivista Musicale Italiana*, Vol. XIV (1907), p. 855.

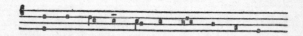

and a *raison d'être* of its own. There is no padding, no tautology, and the added sonority is obtained by extremely delicate, shrewd and dynamic turns of phrase rather than by the combination and accumulation of the parts. The truth is that each of these melodies is essentially vocal, with a tune that finds full expression through the medium of the voice. The acoustic effect and the balance of sound result from a perception of the expressive quality of the melodies; and there is nothing mechanical or pre-arranged about the way in which each part begins and merges in the whole. The academic technique of imitation and canon is felt to be a necessary aid to expression and not a system of formulas. The twenty-five-year-old composer brings his keen and fresh critical spirit to bear upon it, his object being to free it from the icy grip of pedantry and to remove the dross that has formed upon it so that it may shine once more with its original brilliance.

Among the choruses of *La Nave* which were acted in the course of the first performances of d'Annunzio's poem at Rome in 1908 I prefer those of more modest proportions, for in some of the others we find a faint echo of that rhetorical pantomime which pervades Basiliola's poem. Thus, despite the magnificently rich sonority of the processional Chorus for seven voices in the Prologue, which is heard as the Holy Bodies are being carried to the Basilica, and not forgetting the exultant hymn of praise which constitutes the finale, I prefer the thoughtful introspectiveness of the *Inno mattutino dei Catecumeni*, which is as fresh as a silvery dawn over the sea and as clear as the thoughts which the returning sun inspires in young, devout hearts (*Nocte surgentes vigilemus omnes, semper in psalmis meditemur, atque viribus totis Domino canamus dulciter hymnos . . .*—these are the words that are intoned by the two choruses at the beginning of the third episode.) I prefer, too, that other short passage in the Prologue in which, immediately after the mysterious, prophetic voice has echoed from the dome of the Basilica ('Where shall we put our country?'/ 'In the Ship'), the catechumens pray that the sailors may be granted a safe passage and the seamstresses respond from the stage. At such moments the poet, laying aside his prophet's trumpet, has heard the heart-beats of the humble, primitive fishermen and sailors, and the composer has represented them in equally devout and humble colours.

The choruses of *La Nave* are essentially lyrical in conception, as also are those of the *Canzoni corali* (1913-14). Between the two groups stands the 'threnody' of *Fedra*—we have already discussed this opera—in which all the faculties and characteristics to which I have alluded find more powerful and more exalted expression. The tone of *La Rondine* and of the *Canto d'amore* is lyrical and joyous. The former, written for six-part chorus, may be called a hymn in honour of the beginning of spring. It rings with exultation and colourful melody, and its opening bars, popular in style—yet so typically 'Pizzettian'!—all at once open the window on a landscape that is shivering in the last frosts of winter. The rhythm of the *Canto d'amore* is at first sedate. Then it blossoms forth into a fervent melisma, into which the composer has infused a subjective note of sympathy [see page 68].

Per un morto, also for four-part male chorus, is graver in tone and dramatic in character. Tommaseo's few lines of verse—based on a popular Greek original—run as follows: 'Soldiers, dig up the mountains,/and horsemen, dig the fields/that you may bury this youth/on the sea-shore:/let him hear the waves breaking in clouds of spray/and the blowing of the wind/and his comrades/as they cry: "Sails up! Sails down!" ' It is like a fragment of a Greek bas-relief, a swift Homeric scene which the composer has expressed in a melody that develops slowly, ever

more solemnly, with no sudden bursts of movement, every syllable being clearly articulated; there is conjured up a picture of those warriors and heroes with their almost priestlike gestures and their manly grief for their fallen comrade.

Pizzetti has brought the same spirit to his reading of the immortal verses of the Christian funeral rite, and his *Messa di requiem*, in conjunction with which we should consider the *De Profundis*, is the most serene and lyrical of all those with which we are familiar, from Mozart's to Gabriel Fauré's. It has nothing of the sullen, smouldering, apocalyptic tonality that we find in the version of Berlioz, none of the flourishes and violent contrasts which characterizes Verdi's Requiem; and it lacks the classical and rather negative purity of design that is apparent in Fauré's. Its emotion is not expressed in cries and vociferation, nor on the other hand is its warmth dissipated in formal rhetoric. It is a hymn of faith, and that part of it which is directly concerned with the funeral rites is a serene meditation on death. The music is not dramatic in the ordinary sense of the term because it does not set life and death in opposition. Instead, it constitutes a lyrical glorification of the Christian themes of eternal life and resurrection. The city of God is represented as an ideal conception of the earthly city. The composition is for voices only and consists of five parts (the *Requiem*, including the *Kyrie*, for five voices; the *Dies irae*, the most fully developed and, on account of its adherence to the text, the most heterogeneous part of the Mass—it begins in four parts and has eight real parts only at the end, for the very tender *Piè Jesu*; the magnificent *Sanctus* for three choruses, one consisting wholly of female voices, the remaining two of male voices which at one moment sing antiphonally, at another join forces, as in the final *Osanna*; the short, chaste *Agnus Dei*; and the *Libera me, Domine*); all this makes a single entity because of its uniform style. The work was composed in two months (November and December, 1922), and Pizzetti has illustrated each part of the ritual with music whose quality is reflected, as may be seen, in the vocal technique and in the building up of the counterpoint, which is developed to a greater or lesser extent at different stages. The recurring theme of the *Dies irae*, which, as I have said, is the most complex movement, is the soprano and tenor melodic line, which in the course of the piece varies in coloration and meaning [see below], while in the *Libera me* it is the soprano part that is heard above the chanting of the other voices, in descant with them. It produces a most beautiful and moving effect, recalling that of the

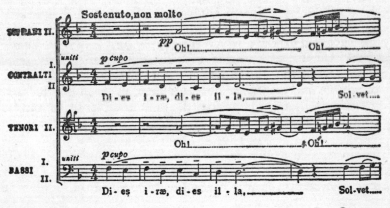

threnody in *Fedra* (in which the voice of Aethra stands out against the monochromatic background created by the other voices) [see page 71]. A similar method is adopted in the *Agnus Dei*, which is one of the most characteristic lyrical episodes in the music of Pizzetti—a veritable gem.

In addition to its use in drama and other forms common to the theatre, the chorus is called upon by Pizzetti to collaborate with the orchestra in symphonic compositions, as in the *Introduzione all'Agamennone* and *L'ultima Caccia di Sant'Uberto* (in the latter it confines itself to uttering an occasional hunting call and a few *hallelujahs* at the end). But in the music which he composed for the *Trachinian Women* of Sophocles it once again performs a function of the first importance. It may, indeed, be said that the dramatic substance of Sophocles' tragedy has been expressed in the music, the resonant sounds of which are heard at decisive moments, reinforcing and prolonging the feelings aroused by the Chorus. The score, which was played for the first time in the Greek Theatre at Syracuse in May 1933, the tragedy being performed in the translation of Ettore Bignone, has a notable amplitude and comprises nine numbers, in seven of which the chorus has a part. The orchestra is remarkable for its unusual organization, *viz.* two flutes, an oboe and an English horn, two clarinets and one bass clarinet, two bassoons, four horns, three trumpets, two trombones and one tuba, tympani, percussion instruments, a harp, six violins, and three double-basses. Clearly, it is an orchestra in which wind instruments form an absolute

majority, but the composer has chosen out of deference to the musical tradition of ancient Greece, not to dispense entirely with the emotional sonorities of the strings, as he had done in *La Nave*. (Here, in the *Danza dei sette candelabri*, the orchestra consists of flutes, oboes, an English horn, a bassoon, a triangle, castanets, tympani, a celeste, and three harps.) An orchestral prelude introduces the tragedy with one of those themes with repeated

71

notes that are characteristic of Pizzetti—ample and resonant
as the fore-court of a temple. I would call it the theme of Heracles,
and would contrast it with the chromatic theme which all at
once is taken up by the wind. Sorrowful, melancholy, and por-
tentous in tone, the latter might be regarded as the theme of the
gentle, hapless Deianira. (In passing I would make mention of
Deianira's 'goodness', which must certainly have found a
particularly sympathetic response in the heart of Pizzetti.)
There follows the chorus of the Epode, then the hyporcheme,
the song of joy at the announcement of Heracles' return to the
Palace of Ceice at Trachis. [See below and following page.]
Beginning in a lively and brilliant 6/8 rhythm, it includes an
intermezzo in a minor key—a portent, as it were, of future
sorrow—and the figure of the queen comes before us in that

attitude of melancholy 'which prevents her from experiencing a full sense of joy even when she has every right to be joyful' (G. Perrotta, *I Tragici greci*, p. 146). The atmosphere becomes steadily darker and more oppressive. The chorus of the first stasimon ('Great and eternally invincible is the power of the Cyprian goddess') is succeeded by the antistrophe of the second ('Come back, come back, O thou who art awaited . . .'); then follows the first announcement of the disaster, the orchestral intermezzo which accompanies the arrival of Heracles half asleep on a litter and the lamentation of the young Hyllus.

73

Finally, the chorus repeats two lines from his last comment: 'The course of future events no man can tell, but for us the present is hapless.' The furious tempest that has been raging in every heart subsides, giving way to serene (but not resigned) contemplation of past vicissitudes. Heracles' invective has died away into a wan smile of death. The hero has surrendered to fate, but not before he has uttered his last cry of defiance and revealed once again the grimness of his heart.

The cantata *Epithalamium*, composed in 1939, marks a return to the lyrical and 'naturistic' atmosphere of the *Concerto dell' Estate* and of the first movement of the Trio. It is an occasional work, in honour of the wedding of a friend's daughter, and was written during a respite from dramatic composition. It is fresh, clear and of a good omen. It draws its inspiration from Nos 61 and 62 of the *Carmina* of Catullus. Pizzetti has preserved first and foremost the spiritual ideas introduced by the Latin poet. He has therefore ignored the sensual and at times licentious implications of the poetry. The work is short and compact in structure. It has the classical form of the secular cantata in which solos alternate with choruses, even if the dividing-line between the different parts is not always clear and full liberty of movement and interpretation is preserved in the adaptation of the airs to the text. It is written for three soloists (soprano, tenor and baritone), a small mixed chorus of eighteen voices and a chamber orchestra comprising thirty-one players. The quality of the work is indicated from the start by the fresh and lively theme for the flute which recurs many times:

The first invocation of Hymenaeus (baritone) is followed by the chorus of the virgins (in three almost homophonic parts). Then the baritone addresses the chosen virgin and invites her to taste the joys of love (*Claustra pandite ianuae*; *Virgo ades...*); this is one of the most felicitous episodes in the cantata. Now it is the turn of the young men, who solicit the favours of the 'nova nupta'. The choral theme is expressed in more virile, more imperative accents, and the tenor soloist also joins in. We see the bride invoking Hesperus and lamenting the fate that is snatching her from her mother's arms:

There follows the soprano aria, in which the vocal melody is constantly accompanied by the solo violin and the flute. The third aria is assigned to the tenor. It is forceful, virile and confident, and the words *Hespere, Hespere* are like a clarion-call of victory. Finally, after an ample commentary by the unaccompanied orchestra, the two choruses combine to sing the praises of Hymenaeus. As the voices, which sound partly through closed lips, slowly die away, we hear the sweet, insistent sounds of the theme for the flute with which the cantata began.

CHAPTER IV

The Songs

THE SONG, WHICH formerly expressed itself in the form of the strophic *Lied*, exemplified in the work of the Schubert-Schumann-Brahms trio, is now also identified with the lyrical prose fragment of the modern French composers (Debussy, Ravel and their imitators). In the story of its evolution the work of Pizzetti asserts itself with a resolute individuality. Having broken down the symmetrical tradition associated with the *Lied*, which was built around a single emotional experience, composers of works for voice and pianoforte have delighted in portraying and analysing different and successive states of mind, according to variations of text, and there has been no nuance of feeling, no attitude of mind, that music has not striven to express, to emphasize, and to intensify. Yet this extreme richness and refinement of emotional content has often led to the dissipation and attenuation of emotivity, and has frequently been the cause of obscurities and breaks in continuity. The continual fragmentation of themes, which have nearly always been reduced to the status of brief melodic episodes, and the incessant variation of tonality, harmony and rhythm are damaging to the stylistic and emotive unity of a composition. Having shaken off the tyranny of the vocal formulas that characterized nineteenth-century melodrama, song has succeeded after much difficulty in creating its own form; and it remains in the majority of cases a fragment of a vaster dramatic whole. We notice this defect in particular when we consider the vocal part, which is often entirely lacking in expressive power. The composer's imagination seems to have restricted itself to creating the instrumental part; and the words merely serve to guide the listener's understanding, providing a criterion by which he may the better appreciate what the pianoforte or the other instruments are playing.

In Pizzetti's songs, on the other hand, the conception is predominantly vocal and the construction, if not strophic, nevertheless in the best examples achieves a unity and firmness that betray the existence of a germ-cell or nucleus around which the piece has been constructed. This may be a theme or merely a rhythmic formula or sometimes a word; but it is always something extremely clear and straightforward. This conception is evident in the very earliest lyrical compositions, in which we already encounter some of the features most characteristic of Pizzetti's work, such as the presentation of the first theme of *Incontro di Marzo* (1904), which is arranged in octaves, and the use of the pedal in *Sera d'inverno* (1907) to create an atmosphere of suspense and ecstatic bewilderment; and it asserts itself in decisive fashion in the lyrical work entitled *I Pastori* (1908), which is deservedly regarded not only as one of the author's most beautiful pieces, but as one of the finest flowers of contemporary lyrical composition. Every moment of lyricism is born of the musical atmosphere created by the opening theme—an ample, protracted theme consisting of nine bars (the last four of which are, moreover, merely a variant of the early ones) and essentially pastoral both in its rhythm and in its arrangement, which seems to suggest the sound of bagpipes:

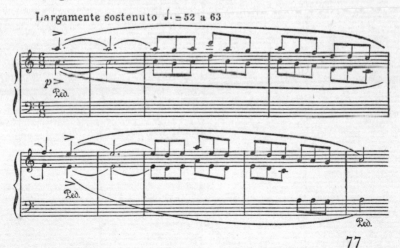

The theme is developed and reiterated in the subdued key of A minor. Sometimes it returns in its entirety, sometimes it is barely an echo, prompted, one might think, by the words. Nor does it become monotonous or tedious, for in its essence it is overflowing with vitality, and it is continually expressing itself in new forms. But however varied and pregnant the theme may be, the nature of the piece is derived from the vocal element, which is charged with emotion at every step and full of melody. Sometimes it is translucent, sometimes it is overcast with unexpressed feeling; but it never degenerates into a cold articulation of syllables or into melisma. One feels that the composer has sung the piece through in his mind before doing anything else (as was the habit of Bellini) and that gradually the poetry has been transformed into melody, which in turn has given rise to the simple but highly sensitive orchestration. But whenever emotion is at its height the human voice is heard unaccompanied, or almost so. The pianoforte confines itself to spinning a fine thread of continuity, and creating a sonorous background.[21]

The same lyrical and vocal conception is apparent in the other four lyrical pieces which were written between 1910 and 1916, but their quality is not always the same. For instance, Pantini's lyrical poem, *La madre al figlio lontano*, is rendered monotonous and, as a result, somewhat melodramatic in quality by a uniform disposition of line and colour which mars the exquisite rotundity of the theme. By way of compensation, what vividness of outline and colour we find in *San Basilio*, with its suggestion of glorious light, the breath of the countryside, and a fresh iridescence that is truly 'edged with silver'! The composer has squeezed the last drop of lyricism out of this Greek popular poem (translated by Tommaseo), recapturing to the full the spirit which gave it birth. There we feel, more than elsewhere— more, that is, than we do in cases where the poetry has already found full and exquisite expression in the verses, as in Petrarch— that the feeling of the moment has been truly and completely re-created. All the nuances of the poetry have been expressed in

---

[21] See the musical accompaniment to the words 'Isciacquio, calpestio, dolci romori...'; also the analogies in *Passeggiata* ('Colmo è il cuore, per nulla rintocca...'), in *Angeleca* ('Che d'è? Meza nzerrata nun vide 'a porta?...'), in the fragment of Sappho ('E l'ora passa frattanto...'), and elsewhere.

the music, as in the accompaniment to Giovanni Papini's *Passeggiata*, in which, though the style is in appearance discursive, centrifugal and almost apathetic, everything gradually converges along interior lines to form the tender conclusion, which is vibrant with passion. The human, fervent poetry hidden beneath the ironical and roguish exterior of Papini's lyric comes to the surface in the music.

But in *Clefta prigione* we already discern the first signs of a leaning towards the drama. It is a compact, powerful piece, in which there is no room for vocal interludes. It is the drama not merely of a man, but of a type and a class. The discursive opening has as its theme the Easter festival. The plaintive interlude, which is also discursive, is full of tenderness, and is characterized by hesitations and reticences. Demo's interruption is brusque and haughty, ironical and explanatory; this is a man who is intolerant of tears. His opening words are full of hope and promise: 'May God and the Virgin grant...' Then he speaks in a soft voice, which grows stronger as he exclaims in vibrant tones: 'Let me take my musket...let me follow the road along the far side of the mountains.' He ends on a note of rising enthusiasm. His dream of freedom and carnage is described in a voice that grows every second more vibrant, resonant and sonorous, and his last two menacing sentences are uttered with emphasis, as though in sympathy with the motions of one who deals heavy and repeated blows.

The two Neapolitan lyrical pieces written during the period when *Dèbora e Jaéle* was taking shape provide an even more positive indication of Pizzetti's trend in the direction of dramatic composition. Because of their compact, synthetic quality and their expressive power the two poems of Salvatore di Giacomo were admirably suited to the task of suggesting two 'studies' for a play. *Angeleca* is the monologue of a drunken man who is staggering homewards after nightfall along a dark alley. He is humming a drinking-song. On the top floor of a small house he sees a lighted window. It is the window of the room inhabited by Angeleca, the woman whom once he loved. Why is this light shining at such an hour? Can it be that the faithless woman has married another, that she is celebrating her wedding-feast—there, before his eyes...? The doorman tells him that Angeleca is

79

dead. 'She's dead,' repeats the drunken man to himself in a dazed, sorrowful voice; and he goes on his way.

As I have said, the composition is in essence important even more on dramatic than on musical grounds; but its importance from the musical point of view is noteworthy. We feel in it the presence of the Pizzetti of the operas—the Pizzetti of *Fedra* and *Dèbora*. Indeed, in a certain sense the two Neapolitan lyrical pieces—but especially *Assunta*—offer us a foretaste of the technique employed in the last-named opera, in particular from the point of view of harmony and orchestration. Naturally, with few exceptions lyrical phrases are no longer in evidence, nor could they be in a declamatory piece that consists of short phrases, curtailed by numerous breaks in the rhythm, in which we detect the restless movement of wills bent on opposite courses of action, and feel them coming into collision and bracing themselves in a continuous exercise of massive power.

Tenderness and hatred, mildness and violence in turn constitute the motifs of *Assunta*, which may, when all is said and done, be regarded as a synthetic drama. But in relation to Pizzetti's work as a whole it is significant above all as an experiment, and its dramatic accents are merely a foretaste or an echo of those found in *Dèbora e Jaéle*, as is clear from the following example [see below].

Written during the same period as the Sonata for violoncello, the *Messa di Requiem* and *Lo Straniero*, that is to say at a time when the composer was in acute distress following the death of his wife, the music for the *Tre Sonetti del Petrarca* belongs to the

*Pizzetti at Locarno (centre) with
Riccardo Bachelli (left)
and the author, Guido M. Gatti*

group of more elaborate works which signalize moments of crisis in the artist's life, moments at which he has set himself problems. The sentiment expressed in the three beautiful Petrarchian sonnets found an ample response in the heart of the composer, but it was a question of respecting a form which was so perfect in itself as not to require, or rather to make impossible, the interpolation or superimposition of any other expressive elements. Faced with such a dilemma, Pizzetti's imagination has conceded too much to his intellect, and his exquisite fidelity to the text has detracted somewhat from the emotional quality of the music. There are in these lyrical pieces moments of lofty poetry—especially in *Levommi il mio pensier in parte ov'era*—but one always feels that the composer's fancy is like a bird whose wings are weighted so that it falls to earth, because the poetic form has a rhythm of its own which he was unable to respect without shackling his own inspiration. The *Tre Sonetti del Petrarca* constitute the only case in the whole of Pizzetti's work in which the musical expression has not re-created *in toto* every expressive element that existed beforehand. Such a procedure is always apparent in those lyrics which Pizzetti has written himself and in those others, popular in character, which he has moulded to suit his requirements. It is apparent in the three *Canzoni* for voice and string quartet and in the *Tre Canti Greci*. These lyrics resemble matter in its raw state. They abound in unadulterated sentiments and bright, colourful images which, though they display an intermittent brilliance that compels attention, do not yet constitute a coherent organism. Often it has been one of these images that has attracted the composer and suggested an entire composition, even if the main theme has not brought it into full prominence. It is so with the end of *Donna lombarda* ('And for love of the King of France I shall die, ah, I shall die'); with the half-tender, half-vulgar 'moral' of *Pesca dell'anello*, the whole of which is compressed into the vocal part; with the abrupt brutal ending of *Augurio*; and with the unusually effective fugue in the *Canzone per Ballo*, a composition which, though it is, as it were, packed tightly into a frame of polished steel, has as much variety, as much light and shade, as a black and white design.

Pizzetti's achievement in the *genre* of the song has been enriched in recent years by other valuable and outstandingly interesting experiments, such as the *Due poesie di Ungaretti* for baritone, violin, viola, violoncello and pianoforte. Here the composer, though adapting his technique to the elliptical character of the language and the hermetic form of the original poems, has not forgotten to stress the more or less fleeting allusions to the idea of 'humanity laid bare' and the pathos which underlies the poet's inspiration. The *Tre liriche* (written in 1944), which constitute the last instalment of Pizzetti's thirty years' output of songs, reveal a tranquillity and a sense of devout spirituality which once again are seen to be essential features of his artistic make-up.

CHAPTER V

The Chamber Music

THE EVOLUTION OF Pizzetti's style conforms in his chamber-music to a pattern identical with that which we noted in his vocal and operatic compositions, and I am accordingly prompted once again to excuse myself for the empirical system of classification I have adopted in describing his work, which is homogeneous and concentrated about a central nucleus in an almost unique degree. As in the vocal work, both solo and choral, so in the instrumental music, we pass from the openly lyrical αἴσθησις of the first Quartet in A and of the three pieces for the pianoforte to the dramatic conception of the two Sonatas, returning in the Trio and in the second Quartet to a form of expression which is both lyrical and dramatic and which, as I have said, is a sign that the artist has reached full maturity.

If the first Quartet (1906) proves to be, so far as its form is concerned, the unseasoned work of a young man, in spirit it contains the germ of everything that Pizzetti was to write in after years. How, indeed, can we fail to recognize, as soon as the opening bars are played, that sense of the clarity of nature to which I have referred, expressed in the theme for the viola, to which the *arpeggi* of the first violin provide an accompaniment of a popular character? And as we listen to the repetitive melodic phrases in the second movement, we cannot but perceive their kinship with those which are frequently introduced into later works as a device to express as it were the throbbing of the heart when passion is at its height. Again, can we deny the common origin of the theme—expounded by the string quartet playing in unison—with which the finale of the Quartet begins and of that which is present in the third movement of the Trio? Or the fact that the composer once again assigns an expressive function to his melodic imitation, which were to become rules of technique in the hands of his slavish followers? One is tempted to say that this youthful work embodies the essence of Pizzetti. If it is characterized by a pardonable naivety and immaturity, it is fresh and suggestive and endued with the grace that befits the age at which it was composed. But consider the theme with variations (third movement). To what uses would it not have been put by any other young man fresh from the academy and a teacher into the bargain? Almost certainly he would have turned it into an exercise in contrapuntal virtuosity and rhythmic gymnastics, or taken as his exclusive model examples of quartet writing furnished by those *fin de siècle* Italian composers who made it their business to imitate the German Romantics, nobly deluding themselves that they were creating the new Italian instrumental style. (And in the eyes of such a serious artist as Pizzetti they must have represented merely a feature of the desert which the Italian concerted music of those days resembled.) Pizzetti instead simply sketched four pictures of everyday life, adhering to the poetic form that does not rule out a rigorous method, namely song (exposition of the theme, then a dance and a 'lullaby for my baby girl', another dance and a repetition of the theme). The whole of the quartet is full of that intimacy which is especially characteristic of the *berceuse* (a short poem on the joys of home-life). Prunières noted how much more sympathetically the happiness of the domestic hearth was celebrated in this Quartet, with its modest proportions, than in the grandiose *Symphonia Domestica* of Richard Strauss.

During the interval between the composition of the Quartet in A and that of the Violin Sonata Pizzetti was undergoing his varied experience of dramatic work, to which we are indebted for a number of increasingly vital pieces. The Sonata, with the Neapolitan lyrics and the *Ouverture per una farsa tragica*, bears a family resemblance to *Fedra*, and is the precursor of *Dèbora e Jaéle*. It was begun in September 1918, when the fires of war were almost spent, and it was completed during the winter of the following year, when the minds of men were once again becoming susceptible to hope. And indeed its development, from the first movement to the last, seems to be in sympathy with the course of outside events, although, needless to say, its purpose is certainly not to portray the external scene, but the drama that was unfolding in the soul of the composer, who mirrors the suffering and shares the joy of all mankind. In the first movement the disturbed background is created by the pianoforte, with its trenchant theme, becoming more and more harrowing, while the violin, with its anguished interpolations, sounds a note of entreaty, like some weak creature buffeted by the tempest. The two themes develop along parallel but independent lines. This is one of the peculiar features of the Sonata: the two themes are never heard individually first on one of the two instruments, then on the other. (Incidentally, this is a feature of all Pizzetti's instrumental music, and it is due to his way of regarding each individual instrument, even in orchestral passages, as an entity that is clearly distinguished by its timbre and by its particular mode of expression. A theme that has been devised for a certain instrument cannot be indiscriminately entrusted to another except for reasons connected with expression, which are at the root of its change of medium.) After a more tranquil episode, based on a theme with a Gregorian flavour, we find ourselves once more in an atmosphere of stark drama, which will prevail from now until the end. It will become more and more intense and heavy, like a destiny beneath whose bludgeonings the fragile human creature bows its head so that only its subdued sobbing is heard. The second movement bears the title *Preghiera per gli innocenti,* This is the first time that we find such a romantic title in the abstract music of Pizzetti, and we know that the composer has pondered and pondered again before deciding to inscribe it at the head of the adagio of his Sonata. But his decision must have been prompted by a desire to reveal once more that sincerity which has always prevented him from acting contrary to his feelings, even when it would have been to his advantage to do so. The largo originates from a theme—the first theme for the pianoforte, in 3/2 time—which has been running through the composer's head together with these words of prayer: 'O Lord God, have pity on all the innocent folk who know not why they have to suffer.'

85

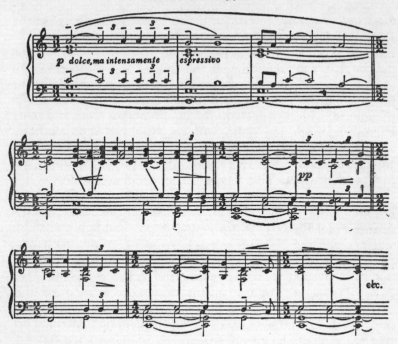

It is a slow theme in C major, unfolding within the limits of an octave, and with its reiterated notes clearly suggesting a vocal accompaniment, namely that which I have quoted above. (But how many of Pizzetti's instrumental themes seem to imply or to call for a vocal accompaniment that remains unexpressed.) Now the storm is past. The man rediscovers his faith and clings to it with all his strength. The peace which his brothers cannot or will not give him he asks of God, and from his lips there issue the sweetest and most heartfelt words he has uttered since he was a child. In this adagio the composer seems to be no longer preoccupied with form. The construction of the episodes, the transitions, the repetitions and the contrasts are the true and inevitable outcome of the musical phrasing, which flows in a lyrical stream from the composer's ever-ardent, ever-alert imagination. The whole piece is an example of instrumental declamation. Its rhythm is as free as air, its variety is in no way studied. It has with justice been said that in the *Preghiera per gli innocenti* it is hard to identify the various themes because the whole piece is one theme. The theme in E flat major that inspires the second episode is perhaps the culminating moment of the whole Sonata.

The third movement, which is almost in the form of a rondo, opens with a lively theme, popular in style, and in the course of its development always preserves this rustic character, containing as it does reminiscences of the carnival and occasional snatches of country songs. The only exception is the nostalgic episode towards the end, which is like an echo of past sorrow. The drama ends on a smiling note; it is as if a rainbow had appeared in a sky which has become once again blue and limpid.

Another drama—but this time of an even more intimate and heart-rending kind—finds expression in the Sonata in F for violoncello and pianoforte, which was composed in 1921. Here, so soon after the event, Pizzetti contemplates his grief at the loss of a beloved companion in a spirit of serenity. (This is not the case in the *Lamento* for voice and chorus—written at the end of the previous year—which the composer has never been willing to publish, for reasons that may easily be imagined. It is a bitter and disconsolate piece, in which the tenor recites Shelley's verses, and the chorus repeats the inexorable words of doom: 'No more!...Nevermore!...' It reminds one of the famous, exquisite piece composed by Monteverdi under the stress of a like sorrow: *Lasciatemi morire*.)

The Sonata for violoncello depicts three supreme moments in the emotional experience through which the composer has passed: his grief at the departure of the beloved person, his revolt against destiny, and his purification through the serene contemplation of death. Several characteristic features of the Sonata for violin are again in evidence. The respective functions of the pianoforte and the violoncello are the same as before, the one evoking and, as a critic has put it, describing the events, while the violoncello expresses the actual sufferings of the composer. In the second movement his desperate struggle against a blind fate is represented by broken phrases, cries and laments, with an undertone of menace; but there follows immediately the catharsis: the violoncello raises its lone voice, seeking phrases of hope and comfort,

and the theme of faith, expressed by the pianoforte, challenges man's grief, seeking to mitigate it with its own inspiration and to plant in a contrite heart the seed of a new life, more sublime and incorruptible.

Once the style of the Sonata had been consciously established, it was destined never to change.[22] On the other hand, his spiritual manner—the subject, so to say, of any work of art—shows itself liable to variation. Thus, the *Tre canti* for violoncello and pianoforte (1924) speak words of affection and tenderness, scarcely veiled by a faint suggestion of melancholy, to his daughter on her marriage, and the Trio for violin, violoncello and pianoforte (1925) is permeated with the joy he feels at a newly-found domestic happiness. In this work the melody broadens and develops with a continuity that is undisturbed by pauses or hesitations. The characteristic melancholy patches of colour have disappeared and the sky is serene to the farthest

[22] The term 'style' obviously embraces all the composer's subtleties of technique and his shrewd devices for manipulating the sonorities of the two instruments.

point of the horizon. There are no dark corners; the light penetrates in every direction; we think of a man waking up after a restless, tortured sleep and raising a hymn of thanksgiving to God. The first notes of the pianoforte diffuse a light and warmth such as we rarely find in Pizzetti's work,

and the strings display throughout a vivacity, almost an exuberance, of expression that is a source of joyful surprise. Phrase and counter-phrase succeed one another without a trace of formality, and the whole is sweetly redolent of the country, so that we think of the Trio as an open-air composition—a glorification of the beauties of nature, which find a response in the soul of a happy poet.

The second Quartet—the Quartet in D—was composed
during the early months of 1933, that is to say twenty-six years
and more after the first. To me it seems that the composer has
made a close study of the classical quartets and that this is the
outcome. Here the poetic structure that is typical of Pizzetti
matches the austerity of the composition, and although new
features are incorporated in the themes the latter are true to
type in that they remain essentially lyrical in character. To put
the case differently, themes like that of the first movement,

or that of the scherzo,

reveal an instrumental quality that is something new in the work of Pizzetti. All the parts, down to the smallest detail, have a basic tension—perfect in its transparency yet closely woven. This is especially the case in the first movement, which, with the joyful clarion-calls of the second violins, and the murmurings of the double bass, seems to suggest a crowded hunt through forest and meadow, mysterious shady places and sudden clearings open to the sun. The adagio is a pure musical reverie, in which the thoughts gradually ascend into an almost metaphysical atmosphere as in many parts of the last quartets of Beethoven. It follows a sinuous and variable course, and frequent chromatic changes give it an instability that is perhaps excessive. The finale returns to the motifs and combinations of the first movement and, after steadily increasing in vigour and liveliness, ends with a solemn largo which has the sweet, rich sonority of a chorale.

After more than thirty years Pizzetti has once again made the pianoforte the repository of his intimate confessions, both in the Sonata for pianoforte, which is not to be numbered among his most successful works, and in the *Canti di ricordanza*, in which a theme from *Fra Gherardo* (the one already quoted on top of p. 48) is freely elaborated.

CHAPTER VI

The Orchestral Works

THE FIRST COMPOSITION for orchestra published by Pizzetti comprises music 'for the theatre'. In 1901 he had written an *Ouverture per l'Edipo a Colono*, and this piece pleased Gustavo Salvini, to whom the young composer had dedicated it. Three years later the tragic actor asked him to write the *intermezzi* for the *Edipo Re*, which he proposed to stage. Sophocles' tragedy was performed at the Teatro Olimpia in Milan, but the music, as was natural, did not receive over-much attention, and for twenty years these pieces were forgotten—even, albeit unjustly, by their author. Absorbed in the creation of his operas, Pizzetti no longer thought of the orchestra as a medium in itself, mistress of its own domain; and it is not until we come to the *Concerto dell'estate* (1928) that we find another symphonic composition for concert performance. But can even this *Concerto dell'estate* and the other orchestral pieces that immediately follow it be referred to as pure concerted music? Do they not seem rather to conform to the same imperious dramatic law as the theatrical works, implying in varying degrees a programme in the sense that I am about to indicate, and therefore not constituting a violation of that unity of æsthetic conception which I tried to bring into prominence when I examined the whole of Pizzetti's work in terms of drama? The modern theory that lyrical composition and pure poetry are identical finds confirmation in the music of Pizzetti, whose rigorous conception of drama excludes all possibility of a swing towards a pure, abstract style of music—music that is neither evocative nor descriptive, and as self-contained as the geometrical figure that may be viewed impartially from any angle, namely the circle. In the æsthetic theory of Pizzetti 'pure music' is a term devoid of meaning. Indeed, in his revolt against it he employs all the resources of irony ('pure—with nothing in it' was how he described it in his essay on the Italian music of the nineteenth century). The construction of a sonorous edifice, even with the aid of the choicest materials and the most exceptional talent, does not interest him unless behind the facade are human beings that live and move. Signs of this dramatic tendency are to be found in every one of his compositions, even when it is not openly declared. A theme, fragment or chord never has a specifically musical value: it represents the spiritual features and lineaments of a character whom we see and know by a name if the work is intended for the theatre, and whom we can easily imagine in other cases. Created in an age of *nature morte*, which sees the world as an eternal source of pictorial or sculptural motifs, a vast synthesis of chromatic values and perspectives, the work of Pizzetti expresses a resolute anthropomorphism, a constant orientation towards man regarded as the centre of the universe.

These instrumental pieces are accordingly programmatic, conforming to an internal pattern which does not allow the energies of the imagination to be wasted on episodes and intricate symbolizations, but keeps them focused upon the central motif that was the original source of inspiration. (This faculty of representing and observing a precise dramatic rhythm while maintaining the rigidity of the musical structure and the coherence of the style is peculiar to operatic composers. Wagner and Verdi had it and were often taken to task for it—especially the former—on the grounds that it indicated a subservience to literature and a depreciation of the rightful function of music). They are programmatic and illustrative not in the manner of Strauss, who, both in the rondo and in the variation distinguishes individual lyrical episodes and does his utmost to differentiate them clearly and to analyse them, but, if anything, in the synthetic and fresco-like manner of Weber and Wagner in their overtures, which are genuine symphonic dramas, expounded as concisely and simply as could be desired. If, therefore, in the *Tre preludi per l'Edipo Re* it is impossible to differentiate the successive phases of the tragedy in so far as it is a narrative of events, it will at once be apparent how intimately and perfectly they reflect the development of the characters' feelings. The first *intermezzo* conveys a sense of the tragic fate that hangs over the city of Thebes. The suspense of an entire people as it waits and no longer dares to hope, and a foreboding of the catastrophe—these are the two themes. The first, which is characteristic of Pizzetti, expresses bewilderment and anguish, and is expounded on wind instruments, violins and violas, accompanied by a rolling of the drums and the held notes of the violoncellos and double bass,

while the other is announced on the horns in tones as imperious and solemn as the voice of doom. The second *intermezzo* expresses the suspense and excitement of Oedipus as he prepares to solve the riddle of the Sphinx. A contrast is afforded to the impetuous initial theme by the oboe motif, which is somewhat in the style of *Tristan*. The third episode brings the tragedy even closer. The old manservant has revealed to Oedipus the mystery of his parricide and of his incestuous marriage with his mother, and the blind king, whose children, Eteocles, Polynices and Ismene, no longer suffer him to remain, prepares to leave Thebes for ever. The Eumenides await him at Colonus, where the last sacrifice is to take place. Only the gentle Antigone has pity on him and goes with him. Her affection and his sense of expiation mitigate his grief, and let a ray of light into the thick darkness, physical and spiritual, that surrounds him. The mournful theme, whose weary, threnodic rhythm has been heard throughout the piece, finds more serene expression in the major tonality of the closing bars and the sonorous, liquid strains of the flutes and clarinets.[23]

The *Concerto dell'estate* is Pizzetti's *Pastoral Symphony*. Nearly all his works have their moments of 'naturism'—a term that should be understood in the sense indicated earlier. It signifies the freshness of the earth beneath the first rays of the sun, the warm, impetuous vitality of noontide, the tremulous melancholy and the poignant sweetness of sunset. It conjures up a vision of life in the open air, among open-hearted people who can interpret and understand nature because they love it and feel it not as something extraneous but as a living and beneficent creative power. The sunrise in *Abramo e Isacco* and *Dèbora e Jaéle*, the choral sunset in *Lo Straniero* and the early-morning scene in *Fra Gherardo*, the first and last movements of the Quartet in A, the finale of the Sonata for violin and that of the Trio, the three piano pieces and countless swift and suggestive evocations of the Emilian and Tuscan countryside in the songs: at such moments the artist's heart is filled with tenderness, his brow clears, and his grief becomes less poignant. These are moments of lyricism, when he is aware of the rhapsodist within him. *Rapsodia di settembre* is the title that Pizzetti has given to the third movement of his Trio, not as an indication that its form is any less strict but in order to emphasize the spirit of free improvisation in which it was composed. We should attach the same significance to the rhapsodic tone of the *Concerto dell'estate*, the most serious orchestral work Pizzetti has so far written, in contradistinction to the traditional types of the modern sonata as it has been known ever since Mozart introduced it. The themes

[23] In accordance with the wishes of the composer, who regards it as a rejected work, I refrain from discussing the *Ouverture per una farsa tragica*, written in 1911 and performed only once—at Milan in 1918, Arturo Toscanini conducting. I would merely say this—it is the only one of Pizzetti's compositions that is 'pessimistic'.

95

are at once presented in a complete form, with all their charac-teristic features and implications. They preserve their indi-viduality throughout the development of the piece: the composer does not detach portions of them from their context or resort to other dialectical expedients in order to renew their vitality. The sequence of the various phases determines the manner in which the themes will re-appear. They do so in turn, each time with renewed potency and in a new light, but always in a complete form. The balance of the piece results from the un-varied rhythm of its presentation. We are confronted not, strictly speaking, with a series of episodes, but with a panoramic, simultaneous (in a spatial sense) vision of the whole. The themes are similarly handled in the first movement of the *Concerto dell'estate*, which is crowded yet clearly sustained by the two self-contained themes—one joyous, the other pensive—that inspire it.

The *Notturno* is one of those characteristically Pizzettian pieces whose inspiration is vocal. As we listen to it we seem to hear the clamour and the murmurings of many voices. The finale, founded on the vigorous rhythm of the galliard, offers a fine example of counterpoint when the dance is repeated, while the strings render a melody that is the expression of a feverish zest for life.

Similar in character to the *Concerto dell'estate* though not its equal in merit is the *Rondo veneziano*. In the *Rondo*, which is divided into three parts in the style that characterizes all Pizzetti's works, the expression is less compact and profound, qualified as it is at times by a widespread suggestion of colour and light-heartedness which we have never yet encountered. But the piece does not break new ground; it is not enriched by new features or new possibilities. Rather does it tend to be characterized by effusiveness, as may be seen if one compares the saraband in the first movement with that in *La Pisanella*, and by exteriorization, which made it easy for the choreographer to translate its music into gestures and harmonious tableaux. Pizzetti's inspiration, which is essentially vocal, loses something of its salient characteristic as the orchestration begins to reveal signs of virtuosity. The slenderness of the orchestral element in *Dèbora* is seen to be even more in keeping with the character of the

Stage design for Act III 'Orseolo'
Florence, 'Maggio Musicale', 1935

music, whereas the greater richness and variety of the composer's later symphonic pieces gives rise to dangerous irrelevancies. We find examples of this tendency even in the *Canti della stagione alta* for pianoforte and orchestra (in which we notice besides, especially in the first movement, a certain weakening of the thematic structure and an excessive use of the *cadenza*), but it is no longer apparent in the *Introduzione all'Agamennone* (1931) or in the music for *Le Trachinie* (1932). It seems to me that here, having returned to the theme of Greek tragedy, Pizzetti has rediscovered the deepest springs of his sensibility and creative imagination. I have already discussed *Le Trachinie*. The *Introduzione all'Agamennone* may be regarded as a synthesis of the music which Pizzetti composed for Aeschylus' tragedy before its presentation in the Greek theatre at Syracuse in 1929. It is a vigorous epitome of that tale of passion. Like the music for the *Edipo Re*, instead of representing in symbolic form definite incidents in the action it expresses the essential emotions and hidden motifs of the tragedy; and if we like to think that it portrays here and there characteristics that should be attributed to Agamemnon rather than to Cassandra, we shall nevertheless have to admit that such themes have a meaning which transcends the individual personage and that they form an integral part of the firm musical structure of the piece. This structure may easily be conceived as a symmetrical design centred around the principal episode, which is expressed in the rhythmic movements of the dance. The part played in this piece by the chorus, though restricted to two episodes, is absolutely essential. In the first episode a few voices sing an elegiac theme, a lament that is, as it were, a presage of the impending catastrophe, but in the second the whole five-part chorus gradually adds its weight to the dull throbbing of the orchestra in a wonderfully sustained episode of poise and dramatic power—remember the chorus in the first act of *Débora*—a series of vocalized oh-sounds which at the beginning resemble laments and later, in an increasing degree, cries of torment and horror, excited curses and, in the final bars, exclamations of grief and stupefaction.

I would not wish to do an injustice to the two massive concertos for violoncello and violin, composed respectively in 1934 and

1944, but they do not seem to me to stand comparison with the
Symphony in A,[24] which was written during the first summer of
the war at Siena. Not that they are lacking in originality on the
score of melody—indeed, they contain a number of notable
thematic phrases—for example, this one (Concerto for violoncello, second movement, violoncello solo):

or this protracted violin medody in the Aria from the Concerto
in A:

[24] As the reader will have observed, A major is one of the keys most frequently employed by Pizzetti as the beginning of a piece.

But it seems to me that the symphonic expression is often subordinated to the needs of the solo instrument, and the structure of the two works lacks the rhythmical freedom that it should have in order to match the grandeur of the treatment.

The Symphony in A, on the other hand, is a work of unquestionable significance, epitomizing all that is best in Pizzetti's orchestral music.

It consists of four movements and lasts thirty-five minutes. The composition of the orchestra conforms to the normal pattern: triple wood-wind, four horns, three trumpets, three trombones, a tuba, tympani, percussion instruments, two harps, celeste and strings. The first movement (*andante non troppo sostenuto ma teso*) begins with a soft, rambling, tranquil theme, introduced by the bassoons and horns and then taken up by the other instruments. This becomes more and more lively, culminating in

the *concitato* passage which leads up to another theme—a terse thematic parenthesis, which will play a highly important part in the general development of the movement. It is the first indication of the conflict of feelings, and heralds the struggle, that will shortly commence. It begins softly on the violins, but all at once develops into a battle-cry. It is bandied about from

99

one group of instruments to another and is punctuated by imperious blasts on the horns in a *fortissimo* of singular intensity.

piano ma intenso e incisivo

The first storm dies down and only the memory of the theme remains, expressed in the low reverberations of the bass strings, while the flute timidly repeats the opening motif. A second *concitado* passage, marked by blasts on the wood-wind and brass, is followed by the reappearance of the opening theme, which this time is assigned to the first clarinet, and by a repetition of the second theme in louder tones, which create an air of congestion. This becomes even more marked in the *più calmo* passage, in which the first theme is expounded by the flutes and horns in sweet, sonorous tones that seem to come from a great distance. The music now shows renewed and increasingly marked signs of animation, and after a very brief slow interlude we come to the end, which is characterized by an extremely rapid tempo. The movement, with its swift alternation of calm and violent passages, forms a single entity, self-contained, compact and unbroken.

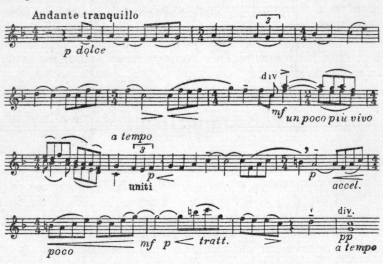

A melody which in the amplitude of its expression and the effusiveness of its sentiment resembles those found in some of Pizzetti's other second movements marks the commencement of the serene andante in F. This melody, which is assigned to the first violins, is played and accompanied by all the strings, the harmonies thus produced being smooth and uncomplicated, in the characteristic manner of the composer [see page 100]. The form of expression is attractive, and although the movement hardly ever becomes emphatic it has its moments of animation. This animation is purely internal: it always subsides quickly so that the atmosphere becomes once again serene and meditative.

The third movement (*Rapido*) is similar in character and function to the scherzo of the classical symphony. The theme is expounded by the first bassoon and the violoncellos, but it is divided and parcelled out among all the instruments.

The alternation of duple and triple time give it a singularly lively rhythm.

In the fourth movement (*Andante faticoso e pesante*) all the constituent elements, both musical and spiritual, of the first three are gathered up anew, condensed and invested with their full meaning. This movement is differentiated from the first—as, for that matter, from the second and third—by its more pronounced poetic tone and its greater compactness of expression. It is a worthy climax to the work.

To the accompaniment of a D pedal, reiterated by the tympani and the violoncellos and sustained by the violins, the oboe expounds, with added emphasis, the initial theme of the Symphony. Partially reiterated by the other instruments, this theme leads up to the March—the essential nucleus of the move-ment—which is introduced by the violas. The bass drum and the tam-tam sounded in turn, combine with the bassoon to form a background, and the volume steadily increases.

Horn notes, growing ever louder and echoed menacingly' and, later, trumpets and trombones, add to the medley of sound' This march is symbolic of some person or thing that no one can stop, a being that crushes underfoot and annihilates everything —a terrible Fate, an inexorable Moloch. Human creatures recoil in terror. Flashes of lightning illuminate the sky, which grows blacker every minute, closing in upon a world in chaos. In vain men try to ward off the danger by prayer. The faint and fugitive accents of the initial theme are expressive at once of an unquenchable desire for tranquillity and peace and of the futility of all attempts to find it. During a breathing-space this theme is heard again on the first horn. It paves the way for the intervention of four violoncellos, which repeat the theme— unforgotten and unforgettable—of the *Preghiera degli Innocenti* from the Sonata for violin.

The quotation is of no special interest in itself, but its appear-ance at this moment makes of it a felicitous point of contact. It is, as it were, an epigraph that in virtue of its conciseness clearly reveals the mind of the artist. With the utterance of the prayer his spirit becomes once more serene; it is illuminated by a new conviction. The initial theme, expounded by the clarinets, with a flute and a trumpet, and overtones supplied by the harp, enlivens the short episode in 3/2 time (*Andante calmo, non lento*) with which the Symphony ends.

CHAPTER VII

Critical Writings

As we read the numerous critical essays that Pizzetti has written between 1905 and the present day—many of them have been assembled in the volumes referred to in the bibliographical note—there is one thing that we realize very clearly. It is that the composer's notable work as a critic is not something extraneous to his creative achievement; its scene is not laid in some remote ivory tower from which he surveys and analyses the work of others; it is, on the contrary, intimately connected with—I would almost say indistinguishable from—his creative output. To say that it precedes his original work, as some have written, is almost as erroneous as the assertion that it constitutes a later or at any rate a different phase of activity. The two elements are so intimately associated that it may be asserted that the artist's qualities are revealed no less by his criticism than by his music. To be ignorant of the first is tantamount to neglecting a most important part, and not merely an aspect, of the second.

The extremely close connection between the two branches of activity—it amounts to an actual fusion, so that it is not a mere relationship between cause and effect or *vice versa*—is due above all to the fact that Pizzetti regards the critical essay as the work not so much of a critic whose object is to make clear and intelligible to others—after making it clear and intelligible to himself—the creative achievement of the artist (including its significance from the point of view of history, culture, etc.) as of a composer who, in the pursuit of an ideal, passes through the experiences of others, reconsiders and judges them as they enter the field of his own experience and knowledge, and tries to see how far they confirm or contradict his personal conception: his purpose being to convert them into fresh material for the enrichment of his own intuitive faculty, to consign them, wholly or in part, to a permanent pigeon-hole and, in the current phrase, to master them.

Pizzetti's critical writings therefore prove to be not merely a source of enlightenment to the reader as he compares the works under review, but genuine essays in self-criticism. They constitute acquaintanceship with artists who may or may not have something in common with the author, and end with a hearty and sincere handshake or a stiff bow; and they form part of the labour of creation that goes on in the composer's spirit. They are critical acquaintanceships such as every great artist has struck up, even if he has not made them public, and they testify to the artist's need for a universal and broadly comprehensive life, open to the four winds of the spirit.

Thus Pizzetti's writings, regarded as a whole, help us in no small measure to understand the art of their author and the æsthetic, and in particular the operatic, ideal which he is striving to realize. Apropos of them one might repeat what Bernard Shaw has said of the best commentaries on Dante and Shakespeare: that they often throw more light on the figure of the commentator than on the subject of his commentary. In addition, one might say of the conclusions and judgements recorded in Pizzetti's critical essays what their author has himself said of a categorical assertion made by Rossini to the effect that the potency of music lies in its rhythm alone. (The conditional and dogmatic character of this assertion is, of course, self-evident.) Pizzetti's comment was that Rossini (and we might add Pizzetti himself), like all true artists, 'did not acknowledge the value of fundamental æsthetic truths unless they could provide him with a justification of the fruits of his creative activity and, so to speak, of the eclecticism of his artistic sensibility'.

But—and this serves to absolve Pizzetti the critic from the charge that has been levelled against him of artistic intolerance and jealousy and of *odium figulinum*—he does not vehemently censure in others forms that are foreign to his own art, nor does he seek to deprecate their use when they seem to him to reflect a conviction, a faith or a conscientious scruple. To cite a single example, it is enough to consider his essay on Puccini (in *Musicisti contemporanei*), one of the sanest and most sensible that has been written on this composer. Though the two men differ in temperament and in their conceptions of art, the study of the creator of *La Bohème* is not violently scathing, nor is it hypocritically destructive. It is, on the contrary, the result of a thoughtful and rigorous examination of the elements of Puccini's art and of the vogue which that art not only made possible, but created and almost necessitated. The author credits the Lucchese composer with a number of felicitous qualities, and when his criticism is directed to certain passages in his works (for instance, the prelude to Act I of *Tosca* and the first scene of Act III of *La Bohème*) it reflects a cordial sympathy and almost a joy at the discovery, after much seeking, of something that stirs the emotions.

Naturally, side by side with the artist—prejudiced, sincere, subjective, and intensely passionate, like any other man—there also exists the composer, able to admire the skill and mastery of the craftsman and to subject his methods to shrewd analysis. But at such times his criticisms lack fervour. It is without warmth. In short, it is not Pizzetti—Pizzetti as he appears to us when we hear him speak of art and life, his voice vibrant with passion, his eyes shining, even while his language remains clear and simple. The pages that relate to composers whose tendencies conflict with those of the author are also shrewd, and abound in subtle observations and in comparisons which suddenly illuminate a whole inner world and an æsthetic system; but they are unimpassioned, and hence their general effect is not always convincing.

The essay on Vincenzo Bellini is perhaps the finest and most profound musical critique that has come out of Italy in our time. It is a critique in the highest sense of the word; that is to say, it is an interpretation and a re-creation of an artistic achievement, is strictly musical without being aridly technical, and is marked by sobriety and beauty of expression. Put it alongside the essay on Claude Debussy or that on Maurice Ravel and, without taking into account the larger scale of the Bellini monograph, you will at once note the differences, which are revealed even in the style, and almost in the choice of words. You will perceive then that Pizzetti has understood Bellini and penetrated right into his mind, whereas he has failed to understand Debussy and Ravel. (The word 'understand', in the sense in which it is here used, means to justify, to be at one with, in an æsthetic, and even more in an ethical, sense, and hence to love. It is therefore unnecessary to add that Pizzetti admires Debussy and Ravel and has been able to estimate their worth as composers, and especially as introducers of new modes of expression into the language of music.) Having reached the end of the essay on the composer of *La Mer*—one might almost say merely of *Pelléas et Mélisande*, since it was this opera, as the reader will already have surmised, that interested the author most of all—and having proclaimed him to be the greatest contemporary French composer Pizzetti finds that there is within him a great spiritual void and that his vision seems blurred. He almost feels that he has lost something of his independence of action as a man after inhaling the subtle perfume of Debussy's music, which produces sweet dreams in the manner of opium. As though to break with his words the spell woven by the harmonies of the French composer and to shake off the torpor that comes over him he hurriedly asks himself: 'But is this, is *this* what art should give us? Is this what we should ask of it—that it should stifle our will to live? . . . Should not art rather exalt life and humanity to a higher plane? . . . Instead of being a destructive influence, should it not be an experience that fortifies the will, an abundant fountain-head of humanity and love?' And the answer is implicit in the question.

So later, when his mind lights upon certain other composers, namely Alberic Magnard and Ernest Bloch, the first of whom is notably inferior to Debussy as a personality, while at the time when Pizzetti was familiar with Bloch the latter had not yet revealed himself as a composer of unmistakable individuality, he feels attracted to them even though he recognizes and unhesitatingly points out their defects. When he examines Debussy's *Pelléas* and Bloch's *Macbeth* in the light of his own conception of drama he cannot help saying that when confronted by the latter he is conscious above all of a feeling of affection and gratitude towards a man who can stir his emotions, whereas when he listens to *Pelléas* he merely has a feeling of great admiration for a most unusual and exquisite artist. These words are at once extremely naive and highly important, even if they will not be forgiven at the bar of musical theory.

In the course of time, as his conception of his art and his awareness of its goal become clearer, his critical scrutiny is transferred from the particular to the general, from the individual work to the general trend, from the artist to his art; and his judgement is influenced to an ever-increasing extent by spiritual and moral values. Twenty years and more of teaching, in the course of which he was in continual contact with young men at the outset of their musical studies, have made the maestro more inclined to gloss over the incidental features of his art, but at the same time more uncompromising and severe in his attitude towards those whom he reproaches with excessive fickleness. While following and preaching the new doctrines he shows scant humility in the face of spectacular novelties and little regard for facile successes. This state of mind—the state of mind of the artist who addresses the young in a broken voice but with his fighting spirit unimpaired—is reflected in his more recent writings, as, for example, the *Lettere ad un giovane musicista*, in which the essential problems of his art are expounded and elucidated with such perspicuity and sanity, or the essay on the performance of music, which affords him an opportunity to reaffirm categorically his belief in the inviolability of the work of art and to condemn all the excesses and aberrations of interpretative taste and misleading criticism. We find again in this essay Pizzetti's favourite assertions, mingled with phrases that testify once more to his probity and consistency. 'Just as creative work demands of the creative artist unremitting, fanatical enthusiasm ... so the interpreter of such work should never perform his task without enthusiasm—nor, for that matter, should the critic. Is this a moral and not an æsthetic question? I know that in the opinion of many the two ideas are distinct and require to be considered separately; but so far as I am concerned they are one and the same thing' (from *Pégaso*, June, 1929). Pizzetti has always believed that no one can be a true artist who is not at the same time a man—a man at heart noble and good, and capable of generous thoughts and actions; and in the event facts have always shown him to be right.

CHAPTER VIII

Conclusion

IF WE CONSIDER Pizzetti's work as a whole and in relation to the fashions that have successively prevailed during the present century we perceive clearly that its fortunes have passed through three phases—the three phases, incidentally, that characterize the fortunes of every artistic creation. To begin with it is welcomed by the intelligentsia, who praise it to the skies, opposing the conservatism of the majority. This is the period of battle and assault, the period of *Sturm und Drang*, when the artists who comprise the vanguard find in the opposition of the masses the justification for their united advance. Little by little the battle grows less fierce, the obstacles less frequent and less formidable. This is the period of slow, peaceful penetration, the period of psychological warfare which finds the ground already broken up and prepared for the planting of the new seed. But the vanguard disperses; its members assert their individuality and in doing so become clearly distinguishable from one another. The wider field of action allows of diversions and enables a variety of routes to be followed. Now the battle is no longer fought for a common ideal. Instead, each fights for himself, indifferent, when he is not envious, to the fortunes of his neighbours. Finally the third phase is reached. This is the phase of maturity and sanity, in which men judge artistic values with minds freed of polemical prejudices and partisan animosities. The work is viewed objectively. It may be great, it may be less than great, but it is always compact and representative of the artist. It is liable to temporary eclipse, but its inner essence, the life that finds expression in it, and the fervour and enthusiasm that called it into being will ensure its survival.

Conclusion

If it cannot be said that the work of Ildebrando Pizzetti has yet entered this 'Olympian' phase, it is not incorrect to assert that it has already outgrown the first two, emerging from them, unless I am mistaken, not merely victorious but with increased vitality. The battle for new ideas has exacted its toll of death, dispersal and wholesale mutilation, but it has left no mark on the work of Pizzetti. The student who, a century or two hence, wishes to assess the extent to which taste varied and musical tendencies fluctuated in our day will not be able to learn much from an examination of Pizzetti's works, in which the *Stimmung* has never varied and the fundamental characteristics of the style have remained unaltered. This is true of the composer's entire output since the end of the last century, and it will probably still be true when he has laid down his pen for the last time.

At the time when Pizzetti made his *début* in the world of art the latest novelty was impressionism: Debussy and his followers were the idols of the majority of the rising generation and music was regarded as the most exquisite expression of the new artistic vogue. But this does not mean, especially so far as Italy is concerned, that everything else was *démodé*; for Mascagni, Puccini, Giordano, Leoncavallo and the other 'realists', were at the height of their fame and popularity. The musical works which were being written in Italy—and I am referring to works by the best young composers of the time—ranged from those in which emphasis of tone and gesture, *à la* Mascagni, and vividness of colour predominated to those characterized by the discreet nod of the head and the nuance (Debussy), save when composers preferred to indulge in academic imitations of the German classical school, following the example of the so-called precursors of the Italian musical renascence which took place between 1880 and the end of the century (Martucci, M. E. Bossi, Sgambati, Sinigaglia). A spectator—he was a student at the time—of the acute crisis that was about to come to a head in the world of music, Pizzetti did not allow his course to be dictated by any of these trends. He felt that, if realistic opera was a manifestation of decadence because it did not completely translate emotion into terms of artistic expression and because it suffered from a superabundance of vitality which could not find expression in the æsthetic spectacle and resembled the inert dregs at the bottom of a glass, impressionism was no less so by reason of a contrary defect, namely an over-refinement and an excess of artistry that little by little excluded the life of the emotions from the work of art, which confined itself to portraying the world of the senses and to spreading a subtle sugary poison which had 'the prodigious faculty of stifling the will to live . . . the faculty of drowning the spirit in nirvana'. He did not yet have a clear mental picture of what he intended to do, but of one thing he was certain—that his work as an artist, whether it amounted to much or little, would not constitute a negation of life: rather it would be, or would aim at being, a whole-hearted, resounding glorification of humanity. He felt that whatever was insincere, or seemed insincere, had nothing in common with art, and that anyone who applauded it not only could not be an artist, but was guilty of sacrilege. 'He who makes art his profession without loving it and believing in it as he might believe in an exalted form of religion is like a priest who says Mass without believing in the sacrament of the Eucharist. And just as more harm is done to religion by one bad priest than by a hundred laymen who neglect their own spiritual lives, so the cause of art suffers at the hands of a bad composer, a bad painter, or a bad poet.'[25]

Though aware that little merit attached to many composers of the past he did not withhold his sympathy from them if he felt that their work was animated by a desire to express a higher form of life than that we know so well and, above all, their faith in their work. In his view the Italian composers of the nineteenth century, from Rossini to Verdi, believed in what they did more or less naively and freely and with a greater or lesser degree of resolution. That is the reason why he loved them and understood them, as he has stated in his recent book on the *Musica Italiana dell'Ottocento*, in which he formulates in unequivocal terms his attitude to the nineteenth century, an attitude that clearly distinguishes him not only from the anti-Romantics (who until lately were legion and are gradually dwindling to a weary handful) but also from those who think they understand the art of the last century because they produce more or less slavish imitations of its forms. The Italian composers of the early

[25] In an address to the students of the Milan Conservatorio, reproduced in *Musica d'oggi*, January 1925.

twentieth century, faced with the mass of operatic music written during the nineteenth century, either gave it their complete approval, admiring it without reserve, or rejected it no less categorically. Few tried to understand it, to feel how much of its lively spirit had been transmitted to the new generation. Pizzetti is to be numbered among those few and must be regarded as one of the shrewdest critics of these works, which in his youth were a source of joy and inspiration to him, as to other artists of his generation. Loving them and studying them, he became convinced that nineteenth-century Italy had not broken with any tradition, but that, rather, a new element had been introduced into opera, something which the previous century had not appreciated—a complete fidelity to life and a moral consciousness which, even where art has not completed the miracle, commands respect. Clearly it is this new factor, in addition to his admiration for this or that opera, that has suggested to Pizzetti his extremely individualistic and in some respects debatable verdict on the nineteenth-century melodrama. This moral force, translated into the dynamic terms of dramatic creation, is something that he feels and admires most of all in Giuseppe Verdi. To Pizzetti the maestro of Busseto is the prototype of the artist-man in the fullest meaning of the term: a man and not a saint, a prey to every human passion and prompt to action, generous but not easily roused to enthusiasm and, as an artist, imbued with a belief in the mission of art to exalt beauty and goodness in all their forms. 'He believed in the passions of his characters. He would not have written a page had he not been prompted by emotion and conviction. He did not pursue art for the sake of amusement. "Amusement," he wrote once, "is a word which in my youth made the blood rush to my head and filled me with a blind fury." ' He felt that Verdi's imagination was fed by sentiments that are deeply rooted in the human spirit—simple, primitive sentiments, which can be understood by all, of whatever country or period. In addition, he felt its presence in the full-blooded operas of the composer's maturity, in which every utterance is a cry and every gesture reveals the emotion in his heart and his eager participation in the fortunes of his characters, who are not phantasms but living beings, not abstractions but creatures of flesh and blood. If *Falstaff* is 'a divinely perfect work, of a supreme, soothing goodness', it is not implied that the famous trilogy of *Rigoletto*, *La Traviata* and *Il Trovatore* is inferior to it. Indeed, one would be tempted to say that Pizzetti's sympathies are more with these compact dramas of love and death than with the comedy of Sir John. Nor could it be otherwise seeing that in all his works there is not a single note of comedy, still less of irony, and that comedy awakes no deep response in his heart, no doubt because it is of its nature somewhat hedonistic and mechanical. Coincidences, misunderstandings, subterfuges, quick-change scenes, and above all the practice of trifling with emotions, falsifying or making fun of them, are undoubtedly a source of pleasure and entertainment, but they are repugnant to a man of the composer's temperament. He loves and admires Verdi because he feels that he loved his characters and that his music does not contain a note which is not inspired by a relentless determination to probe the depths of their souls. To Pizzetti, as to Verdi, action in any form is 'theatre' in the sense that it is dramatic and should result from the clearly defined intuition of a humanity which loves, suffers and fights. (See the systematic elucidation of these and other related notions in the book *Musica e dramma*.) When Verdi wrote his *Messa di Requiem* he was certainly not thinking of the tenets of the Christian faith: he had a vision of man begging for forgiveness, crying out in anguish, trembling at the imminence of divine punishment, and becoming calm again as he hears the words of God. Before his eyes was the drama of all mankind, a drama that continues throughout every moment of human life. Pizzetti is a more cultivated, more thoughtful artist, who has lived in an age more given to reasoning, and as a result his vision is broader; yet it is not hard to discern, even in his non-theatrical work, evidence of his poetic outlook.

I have stressed the natural affinities that exist between Pizzetti and his great fellow countryman, because in my judgement they help far more than is apparent to explain certain features of the former's work. Those who have discussed Pizzettian declamation in terms of Debussy or Moussorgsky, Wagner or Gluck, have failed to perceive that its origin is to be found in the vocal language of Verdi's later operas—*Aida*, *Don Carlos* and *Otello*.

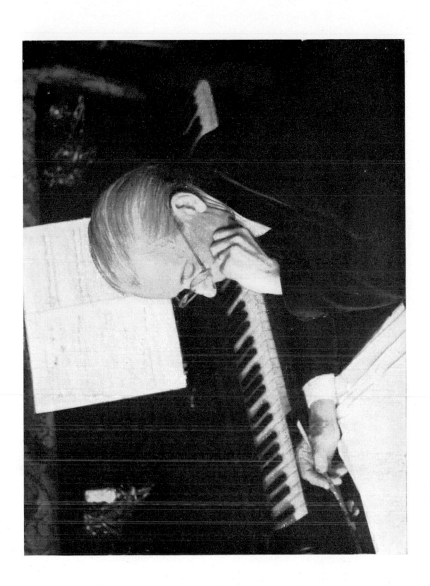

A shrewd young critic of Verdi's work, Massimo Mila, has defined this language as 'a melodious form of declamation which, without sacrificing anything of its basic musical autonomy, does not falsify but rather emphasizes the vital and expressive truth of the words, stylizing material realities in the eternal and fundamental truth of its supreme moments, which the artist's intuition has enabled him to pick out and bring into full prominence.' Pizzetti has understood the lesson of Verdi, but to avoid the possibility of any interruption in the dramatic rhythm has relaxed still further the stringency of the conventional musical form and tried to make his declamation dependent on the words. This was the only way in which he could react on the one hand to the formulas and conventions of the so-called 'Italian theory of vocalism' propounded by Verdi's successors, and on the other to the boundless freedom of Wagnerian melody, which threatened to obliterate those qualities of firmness, clarity and symmetry which are peculiar to Italian art. But little by little the song-form grows freer, the melodies become clearer and more robust, and we see that as his self-assurance increases the artist tends to cast off his self-imposed chains. It is the transition from *Fedra* to *Dèbora*, from *Dèbora* to *Fra Gherardo* and *L'Oro*, from recitative to song, if we may so describe declamation which is as remote in spirit from the high-sounding arabesque style with its rigid and restricted form and its exacting rules as it is from every kind of intoned recitation.

This is the great lesson that is to be learned from Giuseppe Verdi who, without rejecting the past, applied himself to his task, his gaze fixed on an ideal operatic form which the public did not yet believe in, or regarded as the product of other lands and other climes. Today we realize the extent to which Verdi revolutionized musical drama. Between 1840 and 1890, in a matter of fifty years, opera underwent a far greater transformation than it had done during the whole of the preceding century, and there is a much wider gulf between *Nabucco* and *Otello* than between Galuppi's *Il filosofo di campagna* and Donizetti's *Don Pasquale*. Pizzettian opera tends in the same direction. The artist neither disavows the nineteenth century nor wishes to reproduce it, as any present-day composer, after making the most varied experiments, would wish to do. He desires to live through it again in spirit, fully conscious that as a man and an artist he belongs to present-day Italy.

Thanks to the numerous experiments which he has carried out for the benefit of himself and others—were not his culture and his activity as a critic held against him at the time when *Fedra* was first produced?—Pizzetti has a shrewdly analytical knowledge of all the problems of musical technique. Consequently he has never let himself be hoodwinked by the ingenuity of an innovation. Still less has he confused the creation of a work of art with the solution of a problem of technique. This confusion of language, in the sense of poetic expression, with the language of convention is never-ending, and artists are classified almost exclusively according to their contribution to an alleged modernization of the dictionary. Each labours not to create a language *of his own* but rather to enrich a certain stock of expressions that is intended for the use of all, a kind of treasure-house of communal musical works. (It will never cease to be a matter for regret that so much time has been wasted and so much ink spilled by devotees of this idea of a modern musical language made up of formulas, conventional signs and modes of expression forming part of the stock in trade of nearly all composers.) And, as a logical consequence of these premises, there were those who were utterly amazed that Pizzetti could be regarded as a modern artist, and not a few were horrified that in the year of grace 1918, after all that had happened in the world, such a cultivated composer as Pizzetti—I am quoting a critic—could use such a diatonic form of expression (to be precise, the key of C major) without the faintest suggestion of polytonality, which in those days was regarded as a sign of extreme elegance and modernism. Naturally, the same critic finds today that polytonality is *démodé*; indeed, he never fails to pour scorn on it when he comes across traces of it even in present-day music; and Pizzetti, who has placidly continued to employ the diatonic scale, has passed unwittingly into the forefront.

This constant unity of direction makes it impossible to point to successive phases and styles in the work of Pizzetti. One can only reveal how a system of thought and an original poetic theory steadily matured and grew in profundity. Moreover, as I have already had occasion to note, the classification of the composer's works according to *genres*, which I have adopted in order to facilitate their exposition, is strictly speaking arbitrary, for the simple reason that the technical factor and the practical purpose which he had in mind are of little importance in relation to the work as a whole.

A List of Pizzetti's Works

THEATRE MUSIC

1905—*La Nave*. Incidental music for Gabriele d'Annunzio's tragedy, played on the occasion of its first performance at the Teatro Argentina, Rome, in 1908. Unpublished except for the following fragments: *Danza dei sette candelabri* (published by Schmidl, Trieste), *Antifona amatoria di Basiliola* (id.), *Coro dei Catecumeni e delle Cucitrici* (in the review *S.I.M.*, Paris, 1908).

1909–12—*Fedra*. Opera in three acts (Gabriele d'Annunzio). First performed at the Scala Opera House, Milan, on March 20th, 1915, Gino Marinuzzi conducting (published by Sonzogno, Milan).

1913—*La Pisanella*. Incidental music for Gabriele d'Annunzio's drama, played on the occasion of its first performance at the Théâtre du Châtelet, Paris, on June 11th, 1913 (published by Forlivesi, Florence). It has provided the composer with material for an orchestral suite in five parts (1. *Nella Reggia di Cipro;* 2. *Sul Molo di Famagosta;* 3. *Il castello della Regina spietata;* 4. *La danza dello Sparviero;* 5. *La danza dell'amore e della morte profumata*), first played at the Augusteo, Rome, in 1917.

1917—*La Sacra Rappresentazione di Abram e d'Isaac*. Music composed for the performance of Feo Belcari's *rappresentazione* at Florence in 1917, subsequently revived, with an augmented score, at the Teatro di Torino on March 18th, 1926, the composer conducting. In 1931 Ricordi published, complete with orchestral score, the final version of the work, in which the passages that were formerly spoken have also been set to music.

1915–21—*Debora e Jaele*. Opera in three acts. First performed at the Scala Opera House, Milan, on December 16th, 1922, Arturo Toscanini conducting (published by Ricordi, Milan).

1922–5—*Lo Straniero*. Opera in two acts. First performed at the Royal Opera House, Rome, on April 29th, 1930, Gino Marinuzzi conducting (published by Ricordi, Milan).

1925–7—*Fra Gherardo*. Opera in three acts. First performed at the Scala Opera House, Milan, on May 16th, 1928, Arturo Toscanini conducting (published by Ricordi, Milan).

1931—*Agamennone*. Instrumental and choral music, played on the occasion of the performance of Aeschylus' tragedy at the Greek Theatre, Syracuse, in May, 1930.

1932—*Le Trachinie* (Sophocles). Instrumental and choral music, played on the occasion of the tragedy's performance at the Greek Theatre, Syracuse, in May, 1933.

1933—*La Rappresentazione di Santa Uliva* (stage adaptation of the sixteenth-century text of Corrado d'Errico). Incidental music for chorus and orchestra played on the occasion of the first performance of the drama in the Great Cloister of Santa Croce, Florence, on June 5th, 1933, the composer conducting (published by Carisch, Milan).

1931–5—*Orseolo*. Opera in three acts and five tableaux, with two scenic interludes. First performed at the Teatro Comunale, Florence, on May 5th 1935, Tullio Serafin conducting (published by Ricordi, Milan).

116

A List of Pizzetti's Works

1936—*Edipo a Colono*. Instrumental and choral music, played on the occasion of the tragedy's performance at the Greek Theatre, Syracuse. (Unpublished).

1937—*La Festa della Panatenee*. Music for orchestra with vocal solos and chorus, first performed among the temples of Paestum. The following compositions were subsequently adapted from it: *La Festa delle Panatenee*, three pieces for orchestra (published by Ricordi), and *Due Inni Greci*, for solo soprano, chorus and orchestra (published by Ricordi).

1938—*Come vi piace* (*As You Like It*). Incidental music for Shakespeare's comedy, performed during the *Maggio Musicale Fiorentino* in the Giardino di Boboli, Florence. (Unpublished).

1938-42—*L'Oro*. Opera in three acts. First performed at the Scala Opera House, Milan, on January 2nd, 1947, the composer conducting (published by Ricordi).

1942-7—*Vanna Lupa*. Opera in three acts.

ORCHESTRAL MUSIC (for solo orchestra, orchestra and soloist, or orchestra and chorus)

1904—*Per l'Edipo Re di Sofocle*, three symphonic preludes (published by Ricordi).

1911—*Ouverture per una farsa tragica*. (Unpublished).

1913—*La Pisanella*, suite (see *Theatre Music*).

1914—*Sinfonia del Fuoco*. for G. d'Annunzio's *Cabiria*. (Unpublished).

1928—*Concerto dell'Estate*: 1. *Mattutino*; 2. *Notturno*; 3. *Gagliarda e finale* (published by Ricordi).

1929—*Rondo Veneziano* (published by Ricordi). Also performed as a ballet at the Scala on January 8th, 1931, the composer conducting.

1930—*L'Ultima caccia di Sant'Uberto*, for chorus and orchestra (published by Ricordi; also exists in a version without the choral parts).
Canti della stagione alta, concerto for pianoforte and orchestra (published by Ricordi).

1931—*Introduzione all' 'Agamennone' di Eschilo*, for chorus and orchestra (published by Ricordi).

1933-4—*Concerto in C*, for violoncello and orchestra (published by Ricordi). First performed at the Fenice Theatre, Venice, on September 11th, 1934, the composer conducting. Soloist: Enrico Mainardi.

1939—*Epithalamium* (text taken from the *Carmina* of Gaius Valerius Catullus), for solo soprano, tenor and baritone, and a small chorus and orchestra. First performed in Washington on April 12th, 1940; first Italian performance at the Accademia Musicale Chigiana, Siena, on July 14th, 1940, the composer conducting. (Unpublished).

1940—*Symphony in A*, for orchestra. First performed at Tokyo in 1940 (published by Ricordi).

1943—*Oritur sol et occidit*, cantata for bass and orchestra (unpublished).

1944—*Concerto in A*, for violin and orchestra. First performed at the Teatro Adriano, Rome, on December 9th, 1945, the composer conducting. Soloist: Gioconda de Vito (published by Suvini-Zerboni).

1948—*Cantico di gloria: 'Attollite portas'* (from the Psalms) for three choruses (11 parts), 24 wind instruments, two pianos and percussion.

1949—*Canzone di beni perduti*, for orchestra (published by Suvini-Zerboni).

CHORAL MUSIC

1897—*Ave Maria*, for three voices (mixed); *Tantum Ergo*, for three male voices; *Tenebrae factae sunt.* for six voices (mixed) (published by Marcello Capra, Turin).

1913—*Due Canzoni corali :* 1. *Per un morto*, for four male voices; 2. *La Rondine*, for six voices (mixed) (published by Ricordi).

1914—*Canto d'Amore*, for four male voices (in the *Almanacco della 'Voce'*, 1915).

1920—*Lamento* (P. B. Shelley), for tenor and chorus. (Unpublished).

1922—*Messa di Requiem*, for solo voices (from four to twelve): 1. *Requiem;* 2. *Dies irae;* 3. *Sanctus;* 4. *Agnus Dei;* 5. *Libera me* (published by Ricordi).

1938—*De Profundis*, for seven voices (published by Ricordi).

1942-3—*Tre Composizioni corali :* 1. *Cade la sera* (G. d'Annunzio); 2. *Ululate, quia prope est dies Domini* (Isaiah); 3. *Recordare, Domine* (Jeremiah) (published by Suvini-Zerboni).

VOCAL MUSIC

1904—*Tre Liriche* (I. Cocconi): *Vigilia nuziale, Remember, Incontro di marzo*, for voice and pianoforte (published by Schmidl, Trieste).

1906—*Sera d'inverno* (M. Silvani), for voice and pianoforte (published by Schmidl, Trieste).

1908—*I Pastori* (G. d'Annunzio), for voice and pianoforte (published by Forlivesi, Florence). Also for voice and orchestra).

1910—*La Madre al figlio lontano* (R. Pantini), for voice and pianoforte (published by Forlivesi).

1911—*Erotica* (G. d'Annunzio), for voice and pianoforte (published by Pizzi, Bologna).

1912—*San Basilio* (Greek popular poem), for voice and pianoforte (published by Forlivesi).
Il Clefta prigione (*id.*), for voice and pianoforte (published by Forlivesi).

1915—*Passeggiata* (G. Papini), for voice and pianoforte (published by Forlivesi).

1916-8—*Due liriche drammatiche napoletane* (S. di Giacomo), for tenor and pianoforte (originally for tenor and orchestra) (published by Forlivesi)

1922—*Tre sonetti del Petrarca :* 1. *La vita fugge;* 2. *Quel rosignuol;* 3. *Levommi il mio pensier*, for voice and pianoforte (published by Ricordi).

1926—*Tre canzoni :* 1. *Donna Lombarda;* 2. *La prigioniera;* 3. *La pesca dell'anello*, for voice and string quartet or voice and string orchestra (published by Ricordi).

1932-3—*Altre cinque liriche :* 1. *Adjuro vos, filiae Jerusalem...;* 2. *Oscuro e il ciel;* 3. *Augurio;* 4. *Mirologio per un bambino;* 5. *Canzone per ballo*, for voice and pianoforte (published by Ricordi). (There is another version of the ballad *Oscuro e il ciel* for voice and orchestra).

1935—*Due poesie di Ungaretti*, for baritone, violin, viola, violoncello and pianoforte: 1. *La Pieta;* 2. *Trasfigurazione* (published by Ricordi).

1940—'*E il mio dolore io canto*' (J. Bocchialini), for voice and pianoforte (published by Forlivesi).

1944—*Tre Liriche per canto e pianoforte* (published by Forlivesi): 1. *Bebro e il suo cavallo* (Greek popular poem); 2. *Vorrei voler, Signor, quel ch'io non voglio* (Michelangelo); 3. *In questa notte carica di stelle* (M. Dazzi) (published by Forlivesi). (There are also versions of *Bebro e il suo cavallo* and *In questa notte* for voice and orchestra).

A List of Pizzetti's Works

INSTRUMENTAL CHAMBER MUSIC

1906—*Aria in re maggiore*, for violin and pianoforte (published by Schmidl, Trieste).
Foglio d'Album, for pianoforte (published by Schmidl).
Quartetto in la, for strings (published by Pizzi).
1911—*Da un autunno gia lontano:* 1. *Sole mattutino sul prato del roccolo;* 2. *In una giornata piovosa nel bosco;* 3. *Al fontanino*, for pianoforte (published by Williams, London).
1918-9—*Sonata in A*, for violin and pianoforte (published by Chester, London).
1921—*Sonata in F*, for violoncello and pianoforte (published by Ricordi).
1924—*Tre canti:* first version for violoncello and pianoforte; second version for violin and pianoforte (published by Ricordi).
1925—*Trio in A*, for violin, violoncello and pianoforte (published by Ricordi).
1932-3—*Quartet in D*, for strings (published by Ricordi).
1942—*Sonata 1942*, for pianoforte (published by Curci).
1943—*Canti di ricordanze*, pianoforte variations on a theme from *Fra Gherardo* (published by Suvini-Zerboni).

TRANSCRIPTIONS AND REVISIONS

1918—F. M. Veracini; *Sonate* for violin with bass piano accompaniment devised by Pizzetti (in six parts of the *Raccolta Nazionale delle Musiche Italiane*).
C. Gesualdo, Prince of Venosa: *Madrigali* for five voices transcribed into modern notation by Pizzetti (*ibid.*).

FILM MUSIC

1937—Choral and orchestral music for the film *Scipione l'Africano* (C. Gallone).
1941—Choral and orchestral music for the film *I Promessi Sposi* (M. Camerini).
1948—Choral and orchestral music for the film *Il Mulino del Po* (A. Lattuada).

LITERARY WORKS

La Musica dei Greci, a historical and critical study (published by Musica, Rome, 1914).
Musicisti contemporanei (Giuseppe Verdi—Arrigo Boito—Giacomo Puccini —Claude Debussy—Gustave Charpentier—Alberic Magnard— Maurice Ravel—Ernest Bloch—music in the contemporary presentation of Greek tragedy—Trouveres and Troubadours—the musical drama of Christoph Gluck—operatic verse—the oratorio and the sacred drama, *etc.*) (published by Treves, Milan, 1914).
Intermezzi critici (To the memory of Annibale Beggi—the music of Vincenzo Bellini—the immortal *Barber of Seville*—towards a critique of Shakespearean music—the musical interludes in the *Aminta* as performed at Fiesole—the ballad—apropos of Arnold Schönberg and other subjects) (published by Vallecchi, Florence, 1921).
La Musica Italiana dell'Ottocento, in *L'Italia e gli Italiani del secolo XIX* (published by Le Monnier, Florence, 1930).
Paganini (in the series *I Maestri della Musica*, published by Arione, Turin, 1940).

Ildebrando Pizzetti

Musica e dramma (Music and drama—the music of words—'talking in song'—three letters to a young composer—interpreting music—two letters to Ippolito on 'knowing how to listen'—theatre music—Gluck's *Alceste*—Mozart and *The Magic Flute*—the humanity of Beethoven—the art of Hector Berlioz—Meyerbeer's *L'Africaine*—Wagner's *Parsifal*—Moussorgsky's *Boris Godunov*) (Edizioni della Bussola, Rome, 1945).

La musica italiana dell'800 (Letter to Giuseppe De Robertis—nineteenth-century Italian music—the posthumous fortunes of Spontini—the immortal *Barber of Seville*—a Donizetti autograph—the greatness of Verdi—introduction to Verdi's *Messa di Requiem*—the Verdi of 1843 and his collaboration with the public—extract from an 'open letter written by an Italian composer of 1936') (published by Palatina, Turin, 1946).

Various articles in *Il Momento* (Turin) (1903–4), *La Rivista Musicale Italiana* (1906–8), *La Voce* and *Il Marzocco* (Florence) (1909–13), *Il Secolo* (Milan) (1910–1), *La Nazione* (Florence) (1916–20), *Il Pianoforte* (1923–4), *La Rassegna Musicale* (1932–47), *Pegaso* (1928–31), *Pan* (1934), *La Tribuna* (1937–9), *La Nuova Antologia*, etc.

Writings on the Work of Pizzetti

In view of the fact that there has been a notable increase in Pizzetti literature during recent years I think it advisable only to mention writings included in books and a few articles that have seemed to me particularly noteworthy. For the rest I would refer the reader to the bibliographies included in Pilati's study and in the latest Italian dictionaries of music.

G. Bastianelli, *La crisi musicale europea* (Pagnini, Pistoia, 1922); *Ildebrando Pizzetti*, in *Il Convegno*, March–April, 1921.

G. M. Gatti, *'Debora e Jaele' di Ildebrando Pizzetti. Guida attraverso il poema e la musica* (Bottega di Poesia, Milan, 1922).

M. Castelnuovo Tedesco, *Ildebrando Pizzetti e la sua musica corale*, in the November, 1921, issue of *Il Pianoforte*, which was dedicated to Pizzetti and also contained articles by A. della Corte, G. M. Gatti and F. Liuzzi.

L. Pagano, *'Debora e Jaele' di Ildebrando Pizzetti*, in *La fionda di Davide* (Bocca, Turin, 1928).

A. Damerini, *Verdi e Pizzetti*, in *Parma a Ildebrando Pizzetti* (Parma, 1932).

L. Parigi, *Pizzetti*, in *Il momento musicale italiano* (Vallecchi, Florence, 1921).

M. Pilati, *'Fra Gherardo' di Ildebrando Pizzetti* (*Bollettino Bibliografico Musicale*, Milan, 1928).

H. Prunieres, *Ildebrando Pizzetti*, in the *Nouvelle Revue d'Italie*, July, 1920.

M. Rinaldi, *L'arte di Ildebrando Pizzetti*, e *'Lo Straniero'* (Novissima, Rome, 1931).

G. Tebaldini, *Ildebrando Pizzetti, nelle 'Memorie' di G. Tebaldini*, with a preface by A. Damerini (Fresching, Parma, 1931).

G. M. Gatti, *Ildebrando Pizzetti* (Paravia, Turin, 1934).

M. Pilati, *'L'Orseolo' di Ildebrando Pizzetti.* A Guide to the drama and the music (Milan, 1935).

G. Gavazzeni, *Tre studi su Pizzetti* (Cavalieri, Como, 1937).

La Rassegna Musicale, issue for September–October, 1940, dedicated to Ildebrando Pizzetti in honour of the maestro's sixtieth birthday, with contributions by U. Ojetti, G. Gavazzeni, V. Frazzi, R. Paoli, A. della Corte, A. Hermet, L. d'Amico, N. Costarelli and G. M. Gatti.

G. Gavazzeni, *'L'Oro' di Ildebrando Pizzetti. Guida musicale* (Milan, 1946).

Firenze a Ildebrando Pizzetti, including articles by V. Bucchi, A. Damerini, M. Castelnuovo Tedesco, L. Dallapiccola, G. De Robertis, G. Papini and others (Florence, 1947).

Recordings

Tre Canti ad una giovane fidanzata
Aria in D major
    A. Poltronieri (violin) and I. Pizzetti (piano) Columbia D 14556/7

FEDRA
Prelude
    Orchestra of La Scala—Gino Marinuzzi: Telefunken SKB 3202; Capitol 9-86008

LA PISANELLA Suite
    London Philharmonic Orchestra—Carlo Zecchi: Decca AK 1689/90 No. 2 Sul molo del porto di Famiagosta: No. 4 La danza basso della Sparviero; EIAR Orchestra—Willy Ferrero; Cetra BB 25083

Sonata for Violin and Piano
    Yehudi and Hephzibah Menuhin: H.M.V. DB 3579/82

I Pastori
    Margherita Carosio (soprano): H.M.V. DA 5403
    Jolande di Maria-Petris (soprano): H.M.V. DB 6697

Ninna nanna di Uliva
    Rosina Ziliani (soprano): Cetra T 17053

Index

Abram e Isaac, La Sacra Rappresentazione di, 58-60, 95
Aeneas, 17
Aeschylus, 97
Aida, 112
Agamennone, Introduzione all', 70, 97
Angeleca, 79, 80
Antigone, 56
Assunta, 80
Ava Maria, 62

Bartòk, Béla, 65
Basiliola, 66
Bastianelli, 13
Beethoven, 11
Beggi, Annibale, 11, 16, 18, 28
Belcari, Feo, 59
Bellini, 10, 12, 17, 39, 63, 78, 105-106
Bignone, Ettore, 70
Bloch, Ernest, 106
Boris, 39
Bossi, M. E., 109
Brahms, 65, 76
Bruneau, Alfred, 18
Byron, 17, 18

Calzabigi, Ranieri da, 41
Campanini, Cleofonte, 12
Canente (Ovid), 12
Canti della stagione alta, 97
Canti di ricordanza, 91
Canto di Guerra, 11
Canzone a maggio (Politan), 12
Canzoni corali, 67
Canzoni for voice and string quartet, 81
Carmina (Catullus), 74
Castro, Guilheu de, 17
Cavalleria Rusticana, 18
Charpentier, 18
Concerto dell' estate, 92, 95-96
Concerto for violin, 97-99
Concerto for violoncello, 97-99
Consolo, Ernesto, 13
Copeau, Jacques, 56, 60
Corneille, 17, 18

d'Annunzio, 12, 19-24, 28, 56, 57, 65, 66
Dante, 104
Dèbora e Jaéle, 22, 29-40, 44, 53, 54, 59, 64, 79, 80, 84, 96, 97, 113
Debussy, 40-41, 56, 76, 105, 106, 109
De Profundis, 68

Don Carlos, 112
Donizetti, 10, 113
Don Pasquale, 113
Dvorák, 65
Duo poesie di Ungaretti, 82

Epithalamium, 73-74
Euripides, 20
Extase (Hugo), 10-11

Falla, de, 65
Falstaff, 111
Fauré, 68
Fedra, 20, 22-28, 32, 38, 57, 67, 70, 80, 84, 113, 114
Fra Gherardo, 36, 42-44, 46-49, 50, 54, 91, 95, 113

Galuppi, 113
Gavazzeni, G., 52
Gesualdo, 63, 64
Giacomo, Salvadore di, 79
Giordano, 109
Giovanni, Edvardo di, (Edward Johnson), 20
Giulietta e Romeo, 16
Gluck, 40, 41, 112
Grieg, 56

Hippolytus, 20

Il Cid, 17
Il Clefta prigione, 79
Il Filosofo di campagne, 113
Il Sonno de Giulietta, 11
Il Trovatore, 112
Incontro di Marzo, 77
I Pastori, 77-78

La Bohème, 18, 105
La Fiaccola sotto il moggio, 28
La Madre al figlio lontano, 78
Lamento, 87
La Mer, 106
La Navarraise, 18
La Nave, 12, 19-20, 50, 56, 59, 65-68, 71
La Pisanella, 13, 56-59, 96
La Rappresentazione di Santa Uliva, 60-61
Lasso, 63
La Traviata, 112
Lena, 17, 18

Index

Leoncavallo, 18, 109
L'Oro, 51-53, 113
Lo Straniero, 19, 36, 42-46, 64, 80, 95
L'Ultima caccia di Sant' Uberto, 70

Macbeth, 106
Machiavelli, 54
Magnard, Alberie, 106
Manfred, 56
Marenzio, 63
Marinuzzi, Gino, 20
Martucci, 109
Mascagni, 18, 109
Mass for four voices, strings and organ, 12
Massenet, 18
Mazeppa, 17
Mazzini, 38
Mendelssohn, 56
Messa di Requiem, 13, 68-71, 80
Messa di Requiem (Verdi), 112
Midsummer Night's Dream, 56
Mila, Marsimo, 113
Monteverdi, 63, 87
Moussorgsky, 112
Mozart, 68, 95

Nabucco, 113
Norma, 39
Notturno, 96

Orsèolo, 49-53
Otello, 51, 112, 113
Ouverture per l'Edipo a Colono, 11, 92
Ouverture per una farsa tragica, 54, 55
Ovid, 12, 17

Pagliacci, 18
Palestrina, 63
Pantini, 78
Papini, Giovanni, 13, 79
Parsifal, 42
Passeggiata, 79
Pelléas et Mélisande, 41, 106
Peri, 40
Perrotta, 9, 73
Petrarch, 78, 81
Prun, Reginone di, 65 (Tonarius)
Puccini, 18, 105, 109
Pushkin, 17

Quartet in A, 12, 83-84, 95
Quartet in D, 90-91

Racine, 20
Ravel, 76, 105
Reinhardt, 56

Rigoletto, 112
Robertis, De, 13
Rondo Veneziano, 96
Rossini, 10, 17, 104, 110
Ruine di Braunia (Salustri), 12

Sabina, 16
Salvini, Gustavo, 92
San Basilio, 78
Sapho, 18
Sardanapalo, 17
Schubert, 76
Schumann, 12, 56, 76
Seneca, 20
Sera d'inverno, 77
Sgambati, 109
Shakespeare, 16, 18, 104
Shaw, G. B., 104
Shelley, 87
Simon Boccanegro, 51
Sinfonia campestre, 11
Sinigaglia, 65, 109
Sonata for violin and pianoforte, 83, 84-87, 95, 102
Sonata for violoncello and pianoforte, 80, 83, 87-88
Sophocles, 56, 70, 92
Strauss (Symphonia Domestica), 84, 93
Symphony in A, 98-102

Tantum ergo, 62
Tebaldini, Giovanni, 10, 11, 62, 63
Tenebrae factae sant, 62
Tommaseo, 67, 78
Tosca, 18, 105
Toscanini, Arturo, 30, 44, 95
Tre Canti for violoncello and pianoforte, 88
Tre Canti Greci, 81-82
Tre Liriche, 82
Tre prelude per l'Edipo Re, 12, 92, 93-95, 97
Tre Sonetti del Petrarca, 80-81
Trachinian Women, The, 70-74, 97
Trio for violin, violoncello, and pianoforte, 74, 83-84, 95
Tristan, 94

Vanna Lupa, 54-56
Verdi, 10-11, 17, 32, 39, 51, 55, 63, 68, 93, 110-112, 113
Vittoria, 63

Wagner, 10, 23, 24, 40, 41, 93, 112
Weber, 40, 93

Zola, 18